Beautifully
BOSSY

A GUIDE TO SERVANT LEADERSHIP

Beautifully BOSSY

KRISTAL MARKLE-TEMONS

Calhoun Phillips Publishing

Copyright © 2024 by Kristal Markle-Temons.
All rights reserved.

Published by **Calhoun Phillips Publishing,** Mechanicsburg, PA

ISBN 979-8-218-41023-0

Cover photography by Shannon Claire Photography

Printed in the United States of America

www.BossyGirl.org

Dedication

This book is dedicated to YOU. The whole you who knows that you are meant for more. The you who seeks purpose because you know in your gut that you were made for something important. It's from my heart to yours.

This book is also dedicated to my momma, Donna Markle, who walks beside me through it all and is the reason I can love the little girl inside me who was always "just a little too bossy." And to my daddy, Eddie Markle, my angel, who lost his courageous battle with pancreatic cancer on February 13th, 2023. Thank you for always telling me I was special and for compelling me to find out why.

Lastly, to Kianna and Korinna. You girls are my reason for being and my every motivation for making the world a better place. Kianna, you have walked beside me in the most joyous and difficult times. You are wise beyond your years and kind beyond measure. You are beautiful to the world, but I wish you could see yourself through my eyes. You are my angel, and I will always be yours. Korinna, you are a miracle walking on two feet. You have shown me that "Bossy from birth" is a real thing! I'm so proud you are mine and I can't wait to learn how that fire burning inside you will ignite the world with joy and grit! Girls, when we have each other, we have it all. Unbreakable.

Contents

	Foreword	1
	Prologue: Along the Yellow Brick Road ...	3

PART ONE

1	Bossy with a Capital B	11
2	Why Beautifully Bossy Leadership?	17
3	Follow the Yellow Brick Road	25
4	Bossy Values at Work	31

PART TWO

5	My Four Valuable Friends	51
6	Wounded Weslyn	57
7	Perfect Pearl	63
8	Marvelous Mommy	67
9	Amazing Ariel	72

PART THREE

10	The Real Bossy Girl	83
11	The Friends Model	89
12	Who Teaches You Courage?	91
13	Who Teaches You Authenticity?	99
14	Who Teaches You Grace?	109
15	Who Teaches You Bossy Love?	119
16	Integrating Your Authentic Self	127

PART FOUR

17	Breaking the Grip of Fear	135
18	Dropping Our Masks	143
19	Judgment Is for the Birds	153
20	It's Not About You!	173
	Epilogue: My Love Letter to You	183
	Meet Kristal, the Bossy Girl	188

Foreword

The pages of *Beautifully Bossy* have all the feels. It is powerfully inspiring, yet raw and real. It stirs emotions that touch the soul, that push you beyond yourself to do the inner work, to take action to find your powerful purpose and become authentically whole, authentically you. Not everyone has a straight road or a journey that's clearly defined by beautiful yellow bricks. Kristal beautifully conveys this as she walks us through her own complex, personal odyssey, showing us that journeys are full of uncertainty, failure, and windy roads that are sometimes dark but sometimes brilliantly bright. Every road, every path requires work and action. As she states, "This book exists to help women all around the world become authentically whole. It's about healing and growing. It's about deep joy and meaningful sacrifice. It's about pursuing our individual purpose. It's about **owning our power.** It's about ***living lives of love in action*** (leadership)." This is a book about true reflection and growth with actionable steps along the way.

If you are ready to move into action and take that step forward to uncover your true potential and see that fate has always been in your own hands, this book is for you! Kristal will guide you the entire way to help you discover your powerful purpose and show you that you have everything you need to succeed, to thrive, to become confident and beautiful bossy . . . *You've had it all along.*

I am beyond excited for everyone whose lives this book will touch and for the change that will emerge from putting these pages out into the world!

Melissa Gilbo
Co-Founder + CEO
Women's Business League

—Prologue—
Along the Yellow Brick Road...

When a tornado swept Dorothy Gale out of Kansas and dropped her into the Land of Oz, she suddenly found herself far outside her comfort zone, in unfamiliar territory, separated from her friends and family, and forced to stand on her own two feet for the very first time. In Kansas she kept house, helped with the chores, and did all the things that girls were expected to do.

Sometimes, though, she dreamed about what life must be like over the rainbow. And now she was there! Suddenly, she was filled with doubt. Life hadn't prepared her for this. Even as the Munchkins welcomed her to their beautiful country, Dorothy knew that she couldn't stay there. She needed to get home, and her newfound purpose and sense of mission propelled her forward. She had to do something. And she did.

Dorothy took action. She followed the Yellow Brick Road in spite of her insecurities, and, along the way, she met remarkable friends—friends who embodied wisdom, love, and courage—the very same qualities each thought he lacked. They helped her overcome challenges and learn new things about herself. She discovered that she possessed hidden resources of leadership qualities she never knew she had. In fact, you might say she was just a little bit *Bossy*.

In the end, Dorothy's fate was *always* in her own hands. She had everything she needed. She just had to discover it and learn how to use it. She took the journey, learned from her friends, and overcame the challenges. Now, the decision to return to Kansas was hers and hers alone. She was fully in charge of her own destiny in a way that she hadn't been before. She didn't accomplish that by staying in Munchkinland. She did it by overcoming her fears and taking the first step on the Yellow Brick Road.

Now it's our turn. We're all on a difficult journey and the best way to ensure you reach your destination is to do what Dorothy did: TAKE ACTION. You don't need to stay in Kansas anymore, being seen and not heard. But don't stay in Munchkinland either. Read on and take the first step . . .

Prologue: Along the Yellow Brick Road . . .

Kristal, the Bossy Girl

If you get your foot in the door just a tiny bit, you have to kind of wedge it all the way in.
Melanie Perkins

Broken. Bankrupt. Bitter. Belittled. Betrayed. I was bleeding out on the mat. No more bob and weave—just down. Done for. Except, inside me, there was one more fight waiting to be born. I couldn't die here grasping for my salvation, a lifeline, even just a thread. There must be more. As I raised my head, I cringed at the sight of my life splattered before me. Though bloodied and battered, I was still a little bit *bossy*.

At one point, I was the training officer for the largest human services agency in the country with over sixteen thousand employees; then, in one fell swoop, I was reduced to nothing. No one. I was suddenly no longer able to support my little girl. I couldn't take her down with me. I had no choice but to rise. And among the many struggles (which I'll get to), hardship also brought blessings. One of them was a sense of clarity, a clearer understanding of who I was and who I could become. Another was a growing vision, a sense of purpose, the discovery that I have a mission bigger than myself. It was a seed that would grow to form the basis of a movement that would encompass four primary goals:

1. Support women who have experienced challenges, and possibly trauma, so they can become the truest versions of themselves.
2. Provide women with the leadership tools to lead with confidence and own their power.

3. Cultivate a community of women who love and support courageously.
4. Take back and redefine the word *Bossy*.

I honestly have *five* goals, but this last one is personal:

5. I want to leave something for my children so they will never forget who their mother is or doubt the strength that courses through their veins, passed down by generations of strong women who have come before them.

You will learn about my journey and those of my friends in these pages, but more importantly, you will learn about yours. Mine came with a lot of pain and struggle that I hold in my heart as a blessing with the hope that sharing it will lessen the pain of *your* journey.

The Dreaded B-word

I was always the bossy girl. My personality tests say it, my teachers said it, and my family said it too. It never impacted me much to have the B-word used against me—until it did.

Have you ever noticed that when life is good, it's really easy to overlook injustice, bias, and hate? When you are on the protected side of this equation it's awfully easy to look the other way and assume others will fix it for us all. It's easy . . . until your life is on the line. Nowhere is disparity more apparent than in American healthcare.

Once, during a doctor's visit following a severe accident, testing indicated I was in the thirtieth percentile for my overall cognitive functioning. This meant that I could color in

Prologue: Along the Yellow Brick Road . . .

adult coloring books, but was still unable to work, drive a car, or read and write. At the time of the appointment, I had been sitting in the dark for almost six months, and the neurologist congratulated me for "almost reaching the average tier." He said I no longer needed rehabilitation. My eyes squinted with disgust. I was sickened by his measure of my success, and the more he smiled the angrier I got. My Audrey Hepburn grace and elegance disappeared, and I told him, "You don't know me. You will NEVER know me. You will NEVER tell me what I can and cannot do. You can go straight to hell with your testing and your plan. I don't need you."

Do you know what he said back to me? "Well, aren't *you* bossy!"

The truth is that I had been called bossy my entire life, and the older I got, the more I realized it wasn't a compliment. Maybe you've been called the same when you were assertive or forthright, when you tried to take the reins of a floundering project, when you gave instructions or advice, or when you expected nothing less than the best performance from your peers. If these actions make me—or you—bossy, then so be it.

I am bossy (*Bossy,* actually, as we will learn in Chapter One), but I'm alive because of it, and I am also one hell of a leader who loves people relentlessly—always. I am Bossy, but I am also courageous love in action. Today, I am going first. I am going to reclaim and redefine the word bossy. Today, I draw a line in the sand for all of us.

What Is This All About?

I did NOT want to write a book, especially not *this* book. It looks like it's about me, and it sort of is, but that's just the surface. The purpose of these words and these stories is much more important than my personal experience. This book exists to help women all around the world become authentically whole. It's about deep joy and meaningful sacrifice. It's about healing and growing. It's about pursuing our individual purpose. It's about manifesting our potential. It's about *owning our power*. It's about *living lives of love in action* (leadership).

Like Dorothy on the Yellow Brick Road, we are on a journey with a powerful purpose and a clear destination. Together, we will adventure in some dark places, places that may be scary and new. It might feel unsettling. It might disturb others around you. The treasure is stashed in those dark and scary places, and it will take brains, heart, and courage to uncover it. Oz is magical and wonderful, but it can be dangerous. Don't worry; I'll guide you through this journey. Take my hand, and we'll follow the Yellow Brick Road—together.

CONTENT TRIGGER WARNING

This book includes stories of rape, emotional abuse, and domestic violence because they are intrinsic parts of my story. Although no graphic details are provided, readers living with the lifelong trauma created by these situations should practice care when reading.

Part ONE

— One —

Bossy with a Capital B

We call our little girls bossy. Go to a playground; little girls get called bossy all the time—a word that's almost never used for boys—and that leads directly to the problems that women face in the workplace.
Sheryl Sandberg

Why in the world would you want to walk hand-in-hand on such a crucial journey with a woman in her forties who calls herself a bossy girl? I haven't formally introduced myself! Hi, I'm Kristal. I'm not just a bossy girl. I'm THE Bossy Girl. *My purpose is to redefine the word "bossy" so it's no longer used as a tool to silence women's voices or dull their shine.* I'm fully aware of how peculiar it is to call myself (and my company) bossy. It's off-putting. It makes everything harder. Here's the thing: That's okay. The truth is, I AM the Bossy Girl. *Bossy* with a capital B!

My master's thesis was an in-depth study of twenty successful women. Among many other questions, I asked them, and I now ask you: Have you ever been called bossy? Every single one of the leaders in my study said they had been. My guess is you have been too. If not, our journey together may change your answer. If that happens, I hope you will wear it as a badge of honor and a measure of your success!

A Feminist Movement

Redefining bossy is a feminist movement, for sure. But this is a guide leading us in the practice of servant leadership, right? Servant leadership is not anti-men; quite the contrary. Leadership principles are applicable without regard for gender and so is the process of redefining bossy. It's for all of us. These are HUMAN values. Servant leadership and feminism share common goals of fostering empowerment, equality, and inclusivity. They both strive to create environments where individuals can thrive and contribute to positive social change, making them inherently interconnected and relevant to each other.

Our journey through Oz will focus on women because a woman's walk through this world is different than a man's. The word bossy, intentionally or not, is used to diminish the contributions of women who are so bold as to express their willpower and vision for the world. Not anymore. Our work together is changing that.

Let's take a closer look at who gets called bossy. Boys and men are not typically described that way. Those perceived as having masculine energy are not called bossy. We can even consider these masculine folks to be decisive, commanding, in charge, an 'alpha,' or a strong leader.

For feminine folks, it's a different story. If a woman is not properly diplomatic or sensitive, she's considered bossy—or worse. If she pushes too hard the negative perception escalates. She is avoided, not listened to or respected. On the other hand, when female leaders are viewed as friendly, kind, or reasonable, the bias swings the other way. She is considered too sentimental to make tough decisions. It's a lose-lose deal. If we lead decisively, we're bitchy; if we show love and care, we're too soft. Where does this leave us?

It makes a tough job harder. We waste energy in the attempt to balance perceptions, something that our male counterparts do not have to worry about. Success is certainly not impossible. There are many effective female leaders. They are successful despite the conditions, but they are too often exceptions. To fully open the door for *all* women, conditions must change. It starts with our language.

The dilemma doesn't affect only the 'bossy' woman. It's a major factor behind many of society's ongoing challenges, stretching beyond the world of business. It's not just about women's success in the workplace. It's about giving girls a better shot in life. When anyone falls short of their potential, for any reason, it's a tragedy for all of us, and it starts before we are even conscious of the consequences.

Think for a moment about the activities that boys are involved in before the age of 10. What comes to mind?

- Football
- Wrestling
- Soccer
- Karate

How about girls? What do we often encourage them to do?

- Crafts
- Gymnastics
- Dance
- Girl Scouts

What is the relevance of this distinction? I want you to think about the win/lose nature of each activity. At an early age, boys are practicing going after what they want for "the win." (Competitive) Girls are encouraged to grow together. (Collaborative) As a result, girls don't receive the benefit of practice. We don't get the practice of competing or the practice of failing. When boys wrestle, they are held to the ground until they submit, and they must get up and learn that failure isn't personal nor is it the end of the world. They practice taking the hits and keep moving forward.

Over time, women and girls learn that people find us more pleasing if we don't push, but don't hold the group back either. We find ourselves consistently learning to balance our way through the obstacle course that takes us where we want to go. We move forward, but not enough to risk failure. We have limited practice competing and failing. We will compete, but often hold a grudge against our winning opponent because (in our minds) they specifically put us at risk of losing our identity. We move through the obstacle course of life toward the mission, but we are slow and unsteady, resulting in the confidence gap that begins to appear in adolescence and tends to continue into our late 30s.

Girls have never been less talented in the realm of servant leadership, communication, or negotiation. Unfortunately, though, over time the difference in speed remarkably impacts the amount of success women have available. Glass ceiling? Maybe. But it doesn't really matter. What matters is what you choose to do with the resources you have available. What are you going to do? Are you ready to move nimbly through the world with the surefootedness of a young man? You can.

Let's start with one first step. From now on, I invite you to think of the word *Bossy* differently. If you have negative feelings associated with it, I would like you to consider new ones. The next time you are called bossy, I want you to force the internal dialogue of *Thank you!* No defensiveness, maybe no response. But either way, I want you to think *Thank you!* And smile. Now—your feet are under you. You've stepped to the side of the tightrope, and you can run. The Yellow Brick Road is before you and we're going after Oz—together.

— Two —

Why Beautifully Bossy Leadership?

I was once afraid of people saying, 'who does she think she is?' Now, I have the courage to stand and say, 'This is who I am.'
Oprah Winfrey

I am willing to make a bet: You picked up this book because you know something about yourself. You know you're capable of more than what you've achieved. Perhaps you even have a deep-seated sense that you are going somewhere. I'll also guess these feelings are pesky and persistent. They may vary in intensity, but they won't go away. You know there's more inside you, and you can make a bigger splash in this world than you have until now. If you think I'm trying to be Morpheus to your Neo at the beginning of *The Matrix,* you hear me well enough!

The part of you that generates these feelings wants answers. That's why you're reading a book that promises to help you increase your personal power and expand your leadership skills. Maybe you ask yourself questions like, *how do I get on the right path? What holds me back? How do I break free and reach more of my potential?*

We'll explore these questions together later, but for now I have more questions. What if you experienced everything in black and white like Dorothy's life in Kansas—a gloomy, routine, mundane, colorless existence? Dorothy dreams of a life and a world "somewhere over the rainbow." She did this as a young girl—many of us did—and the feeling can persist throughout our lives. I often relate to Dorothy. Do you?

Let's ask that same question a different way: What if, on a scale of one to ten, your Life Energy dial was stuck at three? What if you were stuck at three and you didn't even know it? Did Dorothy know she was living in black and white before she saw the colors of Oz? Would you *like* to know? And if you did, would you want to do something to change it? What would you do to live your life in full and glorious color?

> "Becoming a Beautifully Bossy leader unlocks the magic and wonder of Oz."
>
> Bossy Bit #1

What would you do to turn that knob up to ten and experience greater levels of Life Energy?

I suppose it depends on what comes to mind when you consider the phrase *Life Energy,* but I would guess that you'd do whatever you could to experience more of it. The concepts in this book have the power to do that for you. Go all in and do the heavy lifting. You don't have to do it by yourself, though. That's one of the benefits of the Beautifully Bossy movement. We do this work on and for ourselves, but we do it together because we need each other.

So, what is that work, and what do we get for our effort?

Let's Go Back to Kansas

The real-life State of Kansas has spent well over a century being unfavorably compared to the Land of Oz, so please understand that I mean no disrespect to the state or the wonderful people in it when I say that the fictional version of Kansas is mundane, routine, colorless, uninspired, and boring. It's a great illustration that nearly everyone can grasp, and when we refer to this version of Kansas, we often mean more than just the dreariness that's presented on the surface. Life in the metaphorical Kansas may mean we have thoughts and feelings we are unable to share with anyone. It can mean not being truly close to another soul. Leaders in organizations can feel isolated, without a confidante who truly understands them. We can feel the same sense of isolation in our personal lives. Too often, primary relationships endure for decades without ever achieving deep, uninhibited intimacy. And that's a shame, isn't it?

When we say we're in Kansas, we might also mean we feel somehow depleted. We might feel tired or even exhausted all the time. That state of being is like an energy crisis. We may know what needs to be done, but we just don't have the gusto to do it.

What if, like Dorothy, something came along (hopefully not a twister!) and whisked you off to a completely new world? What if you went through some manner of ordeal, like Dorothy did, in which you lose your sense of where you are—maybe even *who* you are—and you become confused and disoriented? Then, after that short, tumultuous experience, you come to a sudden thudding stop. You gather yourself and step, wide-eyed, into a previously unknown reality. Imagine seeing color for the first time! Imagine never knowing the smell of flowers and suddenly your nostrils fill with the intoxicating beauty of their sweet perfume! What might that be like?

What if you found yourself on the Yellow Brick Road, and you could choose to follow it? What if all the bleakness and loneliness of Kansas is optional? You ARE on the Yellow Brick Road. No matter what you see in your way, or what you feel holds you back, you can follow that shining path right now.

When you choose Oz, you choose color. You choose fragrance. You choose Life Energy. You choose to FEEL. To *really* feel! You get to live your life fully and out loud. It's not all sunshine and roses, of course. There are wicked witches and flying monkeys in Oz. But it's also where you find YOU! It is where you find what's real and lasting about you. It's where you figure out how to better serve others. It's where you learn to get out of your own way and experience true freedom. But remember, growth is not a cognitive exercise. You need to DO something. You need to make an irrevocable, ironclad, no-going-back, all-bridges-burned decision. Are you ready?

YOU are a leader!

What does all of this "Oz talk" have to do with servant leadership? Everything! But wait! What is a Beautifully Bossy servant leader anyway? Servant leadership intertwines the courage of finding oneself with fostering an environment where both personal growth and collective success flourish. Servant leaders use their courage as a cornerstone to propel themselves and others to embrace vulnerability and authenticity in their pursuit of self-discovery. We learn to navigate challenges with resilience, drawing strength from the commitment to serve others. This journey not only cultivates a deeper understanding of oneself but also inspires others to embark on their own paths of growth and fulfillment. In essence, servant leadership fueled by courage becomes a transformative force, making each one of us better tomorrow than we are today—continually out serving one another in the best interest of the mission and the team.

So, I have another question. Do you consider yourself a leader? What's your answer? Go ahead . . . I'll wait.

I notice three types of responses when I ask groups this question.

1. A small, enthusiastic handful raising their hands high.
2. Those casting their eyes to the floor and trying to escape notice.
3. Or the lukewarm, half-raised-hand folks thinking, "I know I should raise my hand, but I'm not really feeling it."

How did you respond? Regardless of your response, I have a goal for you. After you've completed this work, when somebody asks you if you're a leader, raise your hand all the way up to the ceiling. Raise it high and with confidence! And if you already have your hand up, raise the other one too!

Squish—Just Like Grape

I am reminded of a famous scene in the 1984 film *The Karate Kid.* Mr. Miyagi agrees to teach karate to young Daniel LaRusso, but before they begin, he asks if Daniel is ready. Daniel replies, "I guess so."

Mr. Miyagi shakes his head and says, in broken English,

Daniel-san, must talk. Walk on road... Walk left side—safe. Walk right side—safe. Walk in middle, pretty soon, squish—just like grape. Here, karate, same thing. Either you karate do 'yes,' or you karate do 'no.' You karate do 'guess so'—pretty soon, squish, just like grape.

I'm not saying I have the wisdom of Miyagi or you the naiveté of LaRusso. I'm also not saying you'll get beat up or run over by a car. The stakes here are different. They are not physical. They are mental, even spiritual. I'm going to show you some models and maps, tell you stories, ask you questions, ask you to complete exercises, and then ask you to use new tools in your life. It will stir up some mud in your stream. If we proceed with the intention of positive transformation, it will be worth it. If not, you may experience pain and effort without a commensurate payoff. I don't want that for you. Success requires a definite decision. You will own your power *yes* or you will own your power *no*. If you decide yes, don't look back. Complete the work and apply it. If you decide the time isn't right, put this book down. Pick it back up when you change your mind.

Everyone is a leader in some capacity. If you haven't enthusiastically embraced this, it's time to start. I say this because we are going on an adventure of discovery together. Ahead of us lies untold treasure. The treasure is different for everybody, but there are some universals, including feelings of gratitude, joy, and fulfillment.

— Three —
Follow the Yellow Brick Road

To handle yourself, use your HEAD.
To handle others, use your HEART.
Eleanor Roosevelt

Follow, follow, follow, follow, follow the Yellow Brick Road. The Yellow Brick Road laid out the path to the wizard. Dorothy was a leader on a powerful mission of self-discovery who was able to inspire, motivate, and move those following beside her. She led the Tin Man, the Lion, and the Scarecrow through the darkness and their greatest fears to become the best versions of themselves. She is a servant leader with a path, but your path isn't bright and shiny like the Yellow Brick Road.

Each of us is a leader in some capacity, but the journey to *servant* leadership is different. It is overgrown and covered in painful thorns. It's the path less taken—for good reason. It hurts. And real life has no outlined golden path to get there. Enclosed within these pages is a powerful model to support you with the tools to achieve any mission you deem worthy. The model describes the values of Beautifully Bossy leadership and how to become them. This is about who you are. This is all the time. Servant leadership is not about who you are at work, but who is looking back at you in the mirror. This model is your path to a new beginning—paint it yellow and start marching.

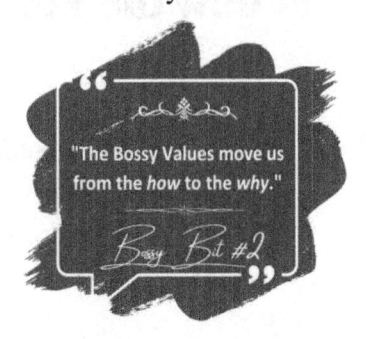

> "The Bossy Values move us from the *how* to the *why*."
> Bossy Bit #2

Let's take a closer look at each Bossy Value:

Bossy Courage. *Doing the right thing in the face of fear.* Courage is not the absence of fear. It is being afraid and acting anyway. It is a choice, a chosen path. The choice comes more easily for some than for others, but that doesn't change the fact that it's the most empowering decision we can possibly make. Courage is the first step in the journey. Really, it's you choosing to use our power to reduce or even eliminate the limiting effects of fear. Bossy Courage is the birthplace of honesty because it allows us to see ourselves clearly despite any insecurities or vulnerabilities. Courage and honesty are the dynamic duo that form the foundation of all other virtues.

Beautifully Bossy Leadership Model

Bossy Grace
Non-judgmental acceptance of what is real in ourselves and others

Bossy Love
Placing others' needs before personal desires

Bossy Authenticity
Your unique fingerprint of attributes

Bossy Courage
Doing the right thing in the face of fear

Choosing courage is the first step toward coming into the light and being seen as our true selves.

Bossy Authenticity. *Our unique fingerprint of attributes.* This is the inner expression of who we are. Physical, emotional, mental, and spiritual—it's the sum of the gifts we receive at birth and how we nurture, shape, and cultivate them throughout our lives. This creates a particular and unique combination within each of us. That's why we call it a fingerprint. It's often messy because it's a constant, painful process of discovering who we are, but the net effect of developing our Bossy Authenticity is that we manifest our potential and thus claim the full extent of our personal power.

Bossy Grace. *Non-judgmental acceptance of what is real in ourselves and others.* Non-judgment is not a lack of standards; it is the willingness and ability to see and appreciate the Bossy Authenticity within ourselves and others. This gives us proper perspective in our decision-making and communication. It converts us from *broadcasters,* primarily concerned with our thoughts and feelings, to *receivers,* primarily concerned with the thoughts and feelings of others. The net effect of Bossy Grace is understanding, empathy, connection, resolution, and an inner calm. Don Miguel Ruiz, author of the classic personal-development model *The Four Agreements,* has a beautiful word for this state of being: *Imperturbability.* Being imperturbable is a sign of advanced emotional intelligence and a hallmark of a Beautifully Bossy leader.

Bossy Love. *Placing others' needs before personal desires.* The word *love* causes a lot of confusion, so much so that I sometimes wish I could call this aspect of the Beautifully Bossy Leadership Model something else. But love is what it is. It's not the *emotion* of love though; that's where the confusion comes in. Bossy Love is an action, not a feeling. It requires skill, emotional intelligence, and all three of the other Bossy Values.

Now that we have defined the Bossy Values, let's turn to the relationship between them and how they work to form a complete leadership system.

Beautifully Bossy Leadership Model

	Bossy Grace	**Bossy Love**
Focus on Others	Non-judgmental acceptance of what is real in ourselves and others	Placing others' needs before personal desires
Focus Inward	**Bossy Authenticity** Your unique fingerprint of attributes	**Bossy Courage** Doing the right thing in the face of fear
	Being	Doing

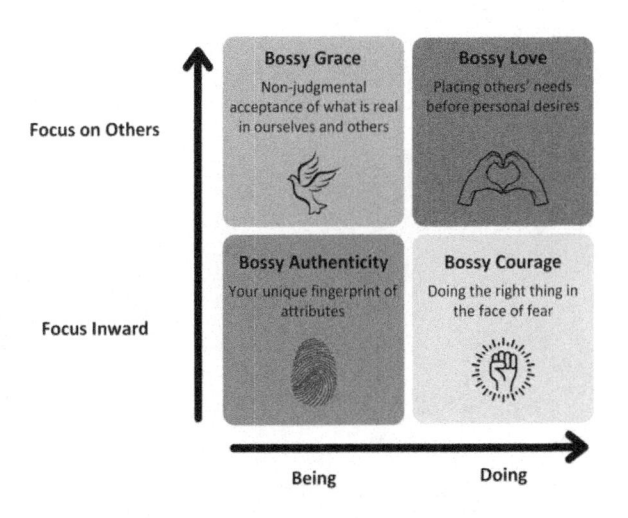

- Bossy Authenticity is a state of mind, focused inward.
- Bossy Courage is an action, focused inward.
- Bossy Grace is a state of mind, focused on others.
- Bossy Love is an action, focused on others.

It is a cycle, one of continuous growth. We're never done. With each ensuing cycle, we become a bit more capable, a bit more dialed in, a bit more Beautifully Bossy. As we intentionally meet the challenges of this process, we naturally bring others along for the journey. In so doing, we help them with their own development. The ability to develop servant leadership skills in others is another hallmark of the Beautifully Bossy leader.

—Four—
Bossy Values at Work

Now that we've covered the **Beautifully Bossy Leadership Model,** let's look at how to use it. We'll further refine the Bossy Values, how to build them, and how they are most elegantly applied.

Bossy Courage

Courage is the most important of all the virtues because without courage,
you can't practice any other virtue consistently.
Maya Angelou

We are all naturally gifted with special abilities. Mine has always been courage, sometimes even irrational courage! I have always been predisposed to action; fear is not typically a factor. This trait serves me well. It allows me to do semi-radical things like call myself the Bossy Girl. But it has somehow always gotten me in trouble. Picture it: eighth-grade Kristal in biology class in 1992. We were learning about the ozone layer, and suddenly our teacher told us that no one in our classroom should worry about AIDS because only gay people could get it. I was floored and nearly speechless—until I wasn't. I stood in the middle of class and told my teacher he was full of shit. I was invited to leave.

Nevertheless, I'm thankful for this gift. I suppose it came from an early belief that I could 'bank on myself.' But even I am not *never* afraid. Like the Cowardly Lion (and like all of us sometimes) I have debilitating fears that I must overcome. The more I did it, the more coping mechanisms I developed. Think of a time when *you* were afraid but took action anyway. What moved you? Why did you take action when at other times you hadn't?

Did you have a mission? The Bossy Leadership Model always starts with establishing your mission. Understanding what you're fighting for is the bridge to taking steps that feel impossible. Whether you are irrationally courageous, like me, or feel you have none at all, a mission is our vehicle for moving forward effectively. Even so, it will be hard, and there will be risks. If you truly choose your mission, it will allow you to embrace the pain of risk-taking. Was opening my mouth worth the cost of getting kicked out of class? You bet it was.

Learning to master fear is important. You have choices. You can quit; you can compromise; you can

Bossy Values at Work

wait and see where life takes you. Those choices are always available but being Bossy means choosing none of those things. It means standing up, speaking out, taking a chance, and risking failure, all in the name of the mission and all in the name of what is RIGHT. Standing up for what's right, defending people who need protection, honestly assessing people and situations, and being bold enough to adjust—that's Bossy. And it's *Beautiful!*

> "Courage is built upon belief in a mission."
> Bossy Bit #3

Great leaders recommit to and reinforce the mission when it matters most. Bossy Courage in action looks like:

1. Cultivating a strong sense of mission
2. Helping others build their sense of mission
3. Having tough conversations about the mission
4. Doing our best and helping others do the same
5. Providing honest feedback

Bossy Authenticity

Authenticity is the daily practice of letting go of who we think we're supposed to be and embracing who we are.
Brené Brown

If you could have any superpower, what would it be and why? The truth is, your unique fingerprint and most genuine self IS your superpower. Your Bossy Authenticity defines your purpose—separate from your mission. You choose your mission, and you will have many of them. A mission is what you intend to DO. Purpose, on the other hand, is WHY you exist. You receive your purpose and you only have one. For some of us, our purpose is obvious. Others live their entire lives uncovering it.

I didn't consciously choose to be the Bossy Girl—I was born this way. When I was three years old, my mother sat me down for a serious talk. "Now Kristy, let me explain something to you," she said. "I'm the mommy and you're the little girl. Now say it to me." I looked back at her and pointed at myself and giggled with delight. "I'm the mommy and YOU are the little girl!"

That little girl had courage—she was even getting in touch with her authenticity—but it would take her decades to truly uncover her purpose.

I'm reminded of the Disney film *Tinker Bell*. Born a 'Tinker' fairy, the kind who fixes things, Tinker Bell enviously sees other fairies making dewdrops, lighting fireflies, and teaching baby birds to fly. Her jealousy jeopardizes the arrival of spring. When she embraces her natural gifts, embodied by her floating hammer, things change.

> "True authenticity is intentionally and consistently choosing to be more of who you *really* are."
>
> Bossy Bit #4

Tinker Bell's authenticity isn't her floating hammer. It's her sassiness, her Bossiness. It is what gets her in trouble in the first place. She doesn't passively accept the lot that everybody else urges her to embrace. She must find her own path. She gets on track when she finds purpose in the application of her natural gifts. As a girl with a 'pronounced' personality, I had a similar experience. Until I found my purpose, I would burn myself and others with my drive. My purpose made me more socially acceptable, more palatable and, most importantly, more valuable.

Bossy Grace

I wish grace and healing were more abracadabra kind of things. Also, that delicate silver bells would ring to announce grace's arrival. But no, it's clog and slog and scootch, on the floor, in the silence, in the dark.
Anne Lamott

In building this model, I quickly learned that grace is one of the most difficult things to define. Typically expressed in biblical terms as forgiveness from God, I wanted to take it a step further to include our interactions with each other. In the two scenarios below, visualize the definition of Bossy Grace, the non-judgmental acceptance of what is real in ourselves and others.

1. You are an accomplished consultant, and you are invited to participate in a high-level strategic planning session for a client. You are a woman, and the others in the room are men. You offer ideas, but the group interrupts you, talks over you, and seems to put greater stock in what others in the room say. At first this annoys you, then it angers you, then you call it out, saying, "You are paying me a substantial fee to be here and contribute. You are doing that because I know things you do not, and I bring an outside perspective. Maybe you should be quiet and listen to what I have to say?!?"
2. Same scenario. This time you listen and observe. You are quiet and take notes while you are excluded and demeaned. In choosing silence, you notice more of the team dynamic. Near the end of the meeting, you are told, "I think that went well, what do you think?" You are prepared, but merely respond with, "What do you think went well?"

Which scenario would you say is Bossy? The answer is the opposite of traditional understanding. Scenario #1 is "bad" bossy. Scenario #2 is "good" Bossy.

The difference between these two scenarios is Bossy Grace. When we are stricken with fear, we need courage.

Similarly, when we make judgments of ourselves and others, grace will deliver us from the outbursts, negativity, and disapproval that can take hold and move us from connection. As courage is unnecessary when there is no fear, grace is unnecessary when there is no judgment. Just as we will never walk through the world without fear, we will never walk through the world without judgment, though it is good to try! Our first step toward grace is imperturbability and acceptance.

Like Bossy Courage, Bossy Grace is a choice of behavior. In scenario #2, it may seem that we are weak; instead, our silence is an opportunity to own our power and the situation. Having grace does not mean we do not recognize the injustice. It also doesn't mean we are a doormat or passive. We instead accept people as they are, even if they have an attitude we do not like. We recognize that others experience doubts, vulnerabilities, pain, and may act from a non-loving place. We do not allow that fact to upset us or throw us off course. Our power is ONLY over ourselves; we cannot change anyone else. But we can foster connection by leaving conversational space for others. When we have Bossy Grace, we invite the opportunity for change and growth in others. Curiosity and

> "Grace turns bossy into Bossy."
>
> *Bossy Bit #5*

connection will present themselves, and long-term influence can develop.

I must confess something about Bossy Grace: Of all the Bossy Values, this is the most elusive one for me. In this, I wish I were more like my mother. She has always been strong in Bossy Grace. I suppose my struggle with grace comes from the natural tension between my passion for giving women more of their personal power and learning to accept the beauty of what is. A person who fully embodies grace is peaceful, internally quiet. This has never come naturally to me.

> "Bossy Grace creates space for growth and understanding."
>
> *Bossy Bit #6*

We need a way to hold ourselves to high standards and to forgive ourselves when we falter. Bossy Grace allows us to forgive ourselves when we simply can't live up to the expectations put upon us by ourselves, our families, and society. Bossy Grace starts with the person in the mirror. Does it really help our cause and our progress when we are overly self-critical? We often permanently label ourselves as "_____" (Fill in the negative label). Have you ever used words like stupid, fat, ugly, unlovable, weak, unsuccessful, washed up, or just a plain old failure when you think about yourself? These words degrade your narrative. They get you nowhere.

Modern society advances the notion that women can and should 'have it all.' The expectation for many women is to be a great mom, a great partner, a great friend, and a great professional—all at the same time—without a hair out of place. This isn't a reasonable ask. It is not a story favorable to Bossy Grace. If you feel your energy and motivation are declining, give yourself a break. It's not your fault.

Grace in this context allows us to accept that priorities shift. We have limited time and energy, and all we can do is all we can do. Bossy Grace allows us to forgive ourselves when we simply cannot wear four hats at once. It allows us to better discern our choices in the moment, explain our decisions to the stakeholders in our lives and, as a result, better extend and receive grace. It's a starting point. It's a way to accept reality in the present moment.

When I ask you to accept yourself and others, does it feel like I'm asking you to give away your power instead of owning it? I'm not. With Bossy Grace, we discern when and how to set boundaries. We are not pushing through the world haphazardly getting our way like a toddler, nor are we allowing others to do that to us. Saying no and creating realistic expectations will co-create powerful understanding while maintaining the safety that is needed to innovate and explore.

Recently, when I was working with one of my favorite clients, the HR director invited me to lunch. I quickly realized that the intention of this meeting was to "subtly" ask that I no longer wear red heels in the building.

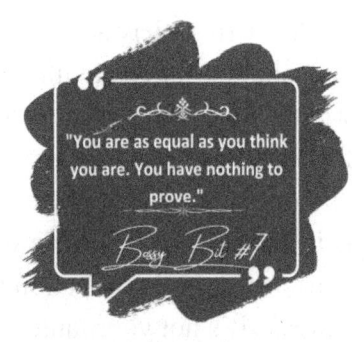

> "You are as equal as you think you are. You have nothing to prove."
>
> Bossy Bit #1

This makes for an interesting situation for the application of Bossy Grace. Red stilettos are the trademark of the Bossy Brand they also in no way impede my ability to complete the mission that I have been hired for – leadership training. I decided that I would not accommodate this request. The answer was no. Is this because I'm faltering in Bossy Grace? Not at all! It's graceful to set boundaries that are mission-critical, like brand consistency. Choosing to set boundaries based on the mission sets a standard that allows us all to know what is okay and what is not okay. Sometimes, setting a boundary and saying no, though uncomfortable, is the most loving, most graceful thing you can do. It may seem counterintuitive, but mutual respect starts with healthy communication that prevents resentment. Boundaries protect the emotional well-being of all involved and prevent situations that could lead to harm and distress. Sometimes the only way to remain Bossy is to hurt someone's feelings, but never because you want to or like to—only because it's mission-critical.

Bossy Love

True leaders understand that leadership is not about them but about those they serve. It is not about exalting themselves but about lifting others up.
Sheri L. Dew

Bossy Love is the vehicle that moves people. It changes hearts. It inspires. It empowers. It is not a feeling. It is an action.

> "Bossy Love is the rarest and most precious leadership attribute."
> *Bossy Bit #8*

Bossy Love is NOT the easy path. It means sacrifice, pain, hard choices, and difficult conversations. Bossy Love often does not feel good. Sometimes it just plain sucks! Unlike the other three Bossy Values, Bossy Love often fails to provide any immediate rewards. There is consistent sacrifice and pain without commensurate payoff. It's almost like working out two hours a day and only eating spinach and seeing no improvement in your strength and physique. Maybe that's why Bossy Love is so uncommon. It doesn't come naturally. It must be taught. It must be consciously chosen.

I made that choice in my mid-twenties. It was hard and painful, but it became the most beautiful and transforming choice I have ever made. I chose to live a life of Bossy Love, though I did not call it that at the time.

Because the concept of love encompasses such a broad spectrum, I think it's important to clarify: Bossy Love is an action, not a feeling. Choosing Bossy Love means sacrificing your own desires for the needs of others.

Bossy Love must be taught. I didn't learn it from my parents, even though I received the most beautiful, unconditional, selfless love from them. I also didn't learn it from friendships or romantic relationships. Believe it or not, I learned Bossy Love from two mentors at work. They called it *servant leadership*.

Mikey had been a master chief on a submarine prior to his career in state government. He was a mountain of a man: six-foot-four, over three hundred pounds, most of it muscle. He intimidated everybody, but he was one of the most loving, amazing people I have ever known. Tragically, we lost him too soon. I am thankful to see that he lives on through the work of the people who were inspired by his amazing heart and commitment to love and service.

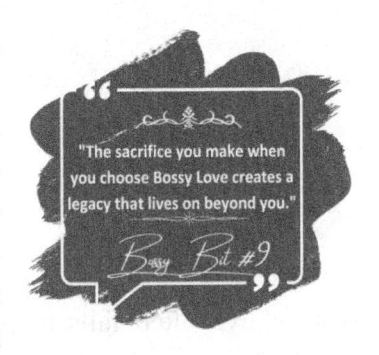

> "The sacrifice you make when you choose Bossy Love creates a legacy that lives on beyond you."
>
> *Bossy Bit #9*

My other mentor, JP, is still with me, and I am blessed to call him my business partner. He was the first person to show me what servant leadership really was. It was ruthless, without condition, and absent niceties.

It involved none of the emotions I had previously associated with love. It was low-key and quiet, but it was also strong and soul-deep. His love revealed itself by giving me what I needed, even when I didn't know I needed it. There would be no Bossy Girl without JP. When I entered the world of JP and Mikey, I thought I was hot stuff. Though I was young and inexperienced, I thought I was exactly what they needed to launch their team to a new level. I knew how to be flashy, and I knew how to use a smile or a coy look to get what I wanted. I am not proud of that. I was in for a rude awakening. JP and Mikey would have none of my 'act.' They were completely unimpressed by my tactics. Fortunately, instead of casting me aside, they showed me Bossy Love and made *me* their project.

Being a servant leader means getting out of your own way, and I was my own biggest roadblock. JP and Mikey had to break me. They called it *ego collapse*. Mikey used military basic-training tactics, repeatedly yelling at me in a way any drill sergeant would envy. "It's not about you!" he would say. The two of them would not allow me to lead or facilitate a group until they saw evidence their message had sunk in.

In retrospect, I was incredibly lucky. We don't get to see love in action every day, so we do not understand it. We think of love as some fuzzy-wuzzy, warm-and-cuddly sort of thing, but love in action is something different, and until you walk beside someone who loves you so hard they would die for you for no damn reason at all, you do not know love in action. You don't learn this by thinking about it. You must experience it, and you must do it.

Here is a small example of how JP embodies love in action. I needed a ride for surgery, and my scheduled transportation left me high and dry. I texted JP at 10 p.m. the night before. He didn't ask how I was feeling. He didn't walk me through options. He didn't ask me to check with someone else first. He simply replied, "I'll be there at 4:30 a.m." He was good to his word—no hugs, no sympathy. He didn't say a word to me on the drive. He was neither put-out nor enthusiastic. It was simply love in action as he, without hesitation, delivered exactly what I needed when I needed it.

I was incredibly blessed to have JP and Mikey come into my life with their life-changing love. If you haven't experienced this yet, don't worry. The amazing thing about the difficult choice of Bossy Love is once you've made it and set an example, something wonderful happens. *It becomes contagious.* When you go first, others follow, and they reinforce your decision. You will feel supported like never before.

I do not mean to imply that Bossy Love will always make life easy. Nope. If someone needs to hear hard truths, I will share them. That's hard. I do it because they need it. I feel bad/sad/like a jerk in the moment, but that doesn't make it unloving; it is the *most* loving. Sometimes giving love in action is painful, but the resulting trust is worth it. Bossy Love is the kind of love that allows us to be pig-committed instead of chicken-committed. The chicken only gives its eggs for your breakfast, but the pig gives everything. Commitment is an amazing thing. The exact moment you make a commitment, things start moving. Commitment is the key that releases the chains that restrict our potential.

Bossy Love is given without the expectation of reciprocity, but there are rewards. People show up for me. When I needed it, I was given support I never could have expected. Bossy Love does not have to be flamboyant, although it's okay if it is. That tends to be my style. I *am* the Bossy Girl, after all! JP's style is unassuming, almost emotionless. Yours will be unique to you. Regardless of personal style, Bossy Love entails respect for everyone, empathy for everyone, effective communication with everyone, courageous conversation when needed, commitment to the cause, and resilience in the face of adversity.

Organizations and families create interdependent communities when Bossy Love is plentiful. Trust is high. Communication is honest. People feel empowered. They are free to try new things. Mistakes and failures are viewed as growth opportunities. Innovation is welcome. The team is aligned, and members are fully invested in their loving community.

Mission, Purpose, Connection, and Community. These are the Bossy Values in action. We become successful and create victories when we use our gifts to shine and overcome. We can also fall and fail when we aren't innately gifted with these values. I've spent a lifetime searching, observing, and learning how to grow and become the best version of myself. As we walk together in using our voices with purpose and owning all of our power, we will further employ each of these values.

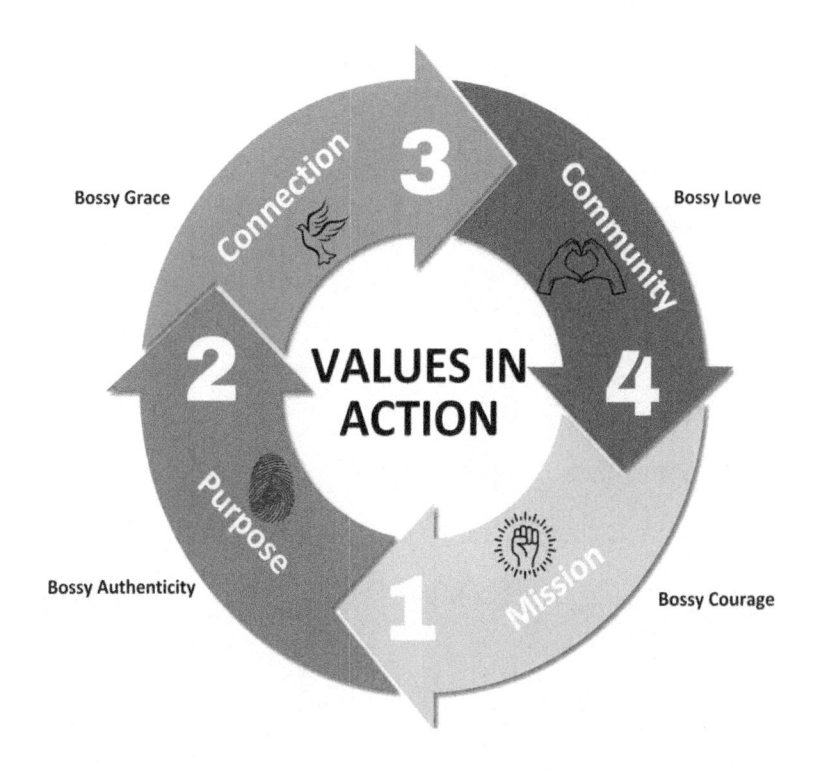

Bossy Values at Work

Bossy Grace — Connection — 3 — Community — Bossy Love

2 — VALUES IN ACTION — 4

Bossy Authenticity — Purpose — 1 — Mission — Bossy Courage

Part TWO

— Five —

My Four Valuable Friends

Owning our story can be hard, but not nearly as difficult as spending our lives running from it.
Brené Brown

Our time together is about to get raw and real. I am going to bare my soul to you and pray my journey helps you to grow in the direction you need most. My guess is you have encountered plenty of pain and challenge. I will share my experiences and those of the people in my life to show you're not alone. I hope to shine a bright light on the path to becoming a Beautifully Bossy leader. Sharing stories of my life that could be looked upon with shame is not easy for me. Even as I write these words, I feel vulnerable and apprehensive. Mainly, I'm afraid some of what I share will cause pain for my loved ones. But if we want to grow, fulfill our mission, and live a purposeful life, pain is unavoidable. It won't be easy for you either. There will be pain. With a grateful heart, I invite you to move forward with me anyway. It will be worth it, my beautiful sister. As we openly share our hearts, we will unlock the true greatness within us—I promise.

On our journey towards Oz we encounter characters who teach us valuable lessons about ourselves. Like Dorothy's Toto, Lion, Tin Man, and Scarecrow, I have friends who have taught me so much about who I am and who I want to be. I would love for you to meet some of them.

First, there's something important I need you to know about these friends. I love each of them, truly, with all my heart. As you discover their stories, you'll see that each one has taught me about a Bossy Value. Yet here is a hard truth about them: these friends have taught me what courage, authenticity, grace, and love are NOT.

Sometimes, my friends amaze me with their achievements, resilience, capacity for love, and commitment to what they want most in life. Other times they share humiliating experiences: suffering, guilt, and irresponsibility. At times, I have pitied them. But overall, I am thankful they are in my life.

My Four Valuable Friends

Weslyn doesn't wear makeup. To my eye, her clothes are tattered, and her hair is always a mess, like she's just been in a fight. She is a little older and a little bigger than me with short, dark hair. If she dressed herself for the part, she'd make a good WWE character—one of those who could take on the guys. Weslyn's hands are always cracked and calloused and scraped. She is pretty fierce, but she can get frazzled to the point of helplessness. It even feels like she's always sick. Have you ever noticed that person who always has that look of fear in their eyes? That's her. She wasn't born fearless, like me, but she would literally sacrifice her life for mine. She teaches me about *Bossy Courage*.

Pearl has got her act together. She is tall and thin. There is never a wrinkle in her ever-appropriate clothes, and she always knows the right answer. Within moments of posting her perfect candids, she has a thousand likes. She maxed out her Facebook friends six years ago and I wish this didn't make me a little jealous. Pearl is the first one to remember how I like my coffee and my love of dark chocolate. She is driven, capable, and successful. She can do anything she puts her mind to. She teaches me about *Bossy Authenticity*.

She may not guess it until she reads this, but I have a friend that I call **Marvelous Mommy**. She is a supermom. Her appearance isn't her focus, but she also doesn't neglect it, because that could embarrass her children. She puts herself together only to the point where she isn't noticeable one way or the other. She wants people to focus on her children. The truth is, though I love and respect Marvelous Mommy, she isn't exactly a great friend. For instance, I love to go dancing. Marvelous Mommy hates that. She never wants to go out or do anything fun. It's all about her kids—ALWAYS!!! Even other children don't much matter to her; she only has eyes for her own. The reality is, though, that she *does* have other responsibilities. And when she attends to them, she suffers from tremendous guilt. She teaches me about *Bossy Grace.*

My friend, **Ariel,** is gorgeous—so beautiful that she gets a mermaid's name for the purpose of this book! She's sexy. She's fun—the life of the party. She is all about living life to the fullest, and she always seeks peak experiences. Her priorities are romance and adventure. She lives on adrenaline and dopamine. She is quite self-centered, so it's best that she doesn't have children. We only hang out one-on-one. She doesn't like the rest of my friends, and they don't like her. She wants what she wants. She teaches me about *Bossy Love.*

Each of these friends has been an important influence on me. By sharing their stories, I hope to inspire you to choose growth and embrace the pain that sometimes comes with change and challenge. Let's take a closer look at exactly how these four women have come to value what they value. More importantly, we will identify how their decisions may influence you as you work toward owning all of your power.

— Six —

Wounded Weslyn

*Fearlessness is not the absence of fear.
It's the mastery of fear. It's getting up one more time
than we fall down.*
Arianna Huffington

Meet **Weslyn.** She might be my favorite of my four friends (Don't tell the others!). Poor Weslyn has walked such a hard road. From her formative years she's faced one ordeal after another, some of which have been life-threatening. It's hard to be courageous when you've been traumatized like that. She does the best she can, but she also shows me what happens when you *don't* have Bossy Courage.

Weslyn's childhood trials came from her grandparents. Like most of us, her parents wanted better for Weslyn than they had for themselves. Their parents,

Weslyn's grandparents, were severe and sometimes cruel. They were judging and critical. Weslyn has often told me about the lifelong impact of overhearing her grandmother saying things like, "What an entitled brat! I can't stand it when she comes here."

As Weslyn grew into a young woman, her grandmother's repertoire of criticisms evolved. "You know, honey, there's a Weight Watchers nearby," or even, "You know those big arms of yours are going to hang down like bags one day." Her grandparents' perception of Weslyn didn't match her own. Once, during Thanksgiving dinner, while participating in their family tradition, she shared gratitude for the gift of her education. Her grandfather stopped the proceedings and told her she wasn't smart enough to go to college, and the only degree she needed was an *MRS*. At Christmases, Weslyn's other grandmother brought gifts for everyone in the extended family, except Weslyn. It was devastating and humiliating.

As an adult (with a degree and career), Weslyn experienced her most impactful calamity. As she waited at a red light, a truck barreled into the rear of her vehicle. Her head slammed into the steering wheel. The trauma to her brain changed her life forever.

I remember how Weslyn was before the accident. She was a loving person, all about the emotional wellbeing of everyone around her. After her accident? It was like the knobs of her emotions were all turned down a few notches. Her everyday life was a struggle. She said she felt stupid, incapable of accomplishing much of anything. She felt lost, a stranger to herself. The feeling horrified her. She was grateful to be alive, and for the supportive people around her, but she felt her dreams and ambitions had been taken away. The change was so profound that it split her life in two—pre-accident and post-accident.

She lost her short-term and long-term memory. She wrote letters backward and could not speak in complete sentences. She also could no longer read the emotional cues of others and experienced seizures and blackouts. It was a tough time to be her friend. Doctors told her she would need to adjust every aspect of her life, but the mundane tasks most of us take for granted posed new and scary challenges for her. She couldn't be in bright light or be exposed to a lot of sensory stimuli. When she was, it would invariably induce a seizure, a blackout, or both.

She has described shopping at the grocery store as feeling like Alice spiraling down the rabbit hole. The sights and sounds, the myriad colors, thousands of items in the aisles, people filling carts and shelves, music and announcements over the PA system—all of these stimuli posed a very real danger. Before entering, she would sit in the parking lot fearing a public blackout or seizure. But she had to go in. Even walking the dog was daunting. She once regained consciousness on the ground in a park, partially covered in snow with her faithful dog on top of her providing warmth and comfort. She has no idea how long she lay there, unconscious.

The parent/child roles were almost reversed in her family. Once she awoke at the bottom of the stairs with her frightened nine-year-old child at her side, on the phone calling for help. And the worst was yet to come.

Especially troubling were the medical issues accompanying a complicated pregnancy – anemia, pain, and bleeding. The doctors were disinterested at best or sometimes even snarky. "Welcome to being a woman," one doctor told her. The bleeding became so heavy doctors thought she would lose the baby or possibly her life. Fortunately, that didn't happen, but even after the child's birth, the problems worsened. She begged her doctors to do anything they could to relieve her suffering. Their answer was a full hysterectomy at only forty years old.

Just a week after her hysterectomy she suffered a headache so excruciating that she had no choice but to return to the hospital. Doctors suspected the worst. The medical staff immediately quarantined Weslyn and conducted a battery of tests. They thought she had bacterial meningitis and told her that she probably had only twenty-four hours to live. Her body had become a prison of pain, but that was nothing compared to the fear that she might not be able to tell her children goodbye before she died. Overwhelmed, she asked, "Does it have to be that long?"

The medical team, donning full PPE, conducted a spinal tap even though they thought she'd be dead before they received the results. Weslyn was lucky. She had contracted *viral* meningitis while in the hospital for her hysterectomy. It tortured her, but it didn't kill her.

Courage does not inoculate us against mental or physical risk. It grants us access to our power. Prolonged pain and repeated trauma can damage us and make us gun-shy. They can make us want to pull back from life to hibernate and heal. Suddenly we are no longer motivated by doing what is right, but by what is safe. We are lulled into complacency, and we become content with the gray of Kansas. We no longer stand against indecency and prejudice and instead become a part of it by default. Weslyn says things like, "I'm not getting involved in this mess" or, "There is nothing I can do to help that."

She's the Eeyore of our friend group—pessimistic and low-key. Because she has overcome such great obstacles, she considers herself courageous. In a way, I guess she is. But not in the way we are talking about. She accepts what the world dishes out and maintains enough strength to survive. But she does not thrive. She has no passion, no sense of purpose. This is not Bossy. This is not Courage. Bossy Courage makes the right things happen. It is not simply surviving as you play the hand you've been dealt.

> "Courage unlocks our personal power."
>
> Bossy Bit #10

—Seven—

Perfect Pearl

I have nothing to hide.
I have nothing to protect.
I have nothing to prove.
I have nothing to defend.
Lisa Nichols

Perfect Pearl is the 'Good Girl,' the 'Chosen One.' You might know someone just like her. She is the standard against whom you measure yourself, but unless you *are* her, you probably come up short!

The more I get to know Pearl, the more I realize she is the product of her need to make people proud. I wonder if she even realizes this about herself. Her parents gave her the world and believed in her in a way that many of us can only dream about. And as I consider what she's told me, I realize it's her love for her parents and her brother and the dynamic between all of them that drives her to please and support others.

Pearl's brother is ten years her senior, and as a little girl she adored her worldly, caring big brother. As she grew, though, she learned that he was getting into trouble. She didn't really know what it was all about, but her mom would cry, her dad would get quiet, and they would all be sad. This was often the state of their family.

Pearl has always known for sure that her brother loves her. She talks fondly of the moments when he taught her to wrestle WWE-style and beamed as she beat children twice her age and size. He would push her through workouts, compelling her to complete knuckle push-ups on concrete blocks until her fists bled. She could do 100 of them, saying the feeling of making her brother proud was worth the pain.

As she grew, Pearl realized that her brother sometimes struggled with being accepted by his peers. He had needed to defend himself, and he prepared her to do the same. She still loves her brother, and he still struggles. Her mom still gets sad, and her dad still gets quiet. And Pearl still can't fix it. This feeling of helplessness has profoundly shaped her.

When Pearl describes herself, she says she was always solidly and powerfully built. Unusually strong, she once challenged her high school's heavyweight wrestler to a bench-press contest. He was making fun of the

Perfect Pearl

cheerleaders who wanted to work out with weights. She is still proud when speaking of her victory! As a cheerleader, she could lift the other girls with much more ease than they could lift her, and, initially, she never felt bad about any of this.

As the head cheerleader, she wanted to date the quarterback. He wasn't interested. He wanted to date the small girls at the top of the pyramid, not the strong ones at the base. She learned that sometimes her powerful physique was an impediment to getting what she wanted. Societal standards, against which she was powerless, shaped who she became.

She could not change the sadness in her family or her physique, but she will never accept feeling 'less than.' Pearl lives up to every standard she imposes upon herself. Approaching forty, she looks more beautiful than ever. Any quarterback would be happy to have her.

Pearl believes the most important thing in life is to not disappoint people. This thought is based in truth, but only when used judiciously. Her drive to succeed leads her to go the extra mile for all the wrong reasons. She not only avoids disappointing others but goes out of her way to positively impress them. She is comfortable with achievement and uncomfortable with failure. She focuses on how others see her. It keeps her from listening to what is real and lasting about herself. She is too focused on getting things exactly right and trying to control outcomes. While high standards and doing our best are success qualities, we must leave room for the contributions of others, avoid obsessing about every little detail, and be ready and able to show our vulnerabilities and shortcomings. Leaders should not strive to be seen as perfect.

I introduced you to Perfect Pearl because she teaches me about authenticity. She teaches me about what authenticity is NOT. Authenticity embraces our unique attributes, our perfectly imperfect fingerprints. Authenticity does not wear the mask of perfection. It does not hide. It does not compare. It does not believe the grass is greener on the other side. Perfect Pearl is lost in Oz with no hope of ever really discovering the true gift of authenticity.

> "Authenticity is not preoccupied with how others perceive you."
> *Bossy Bit #11*

> "Wearing masks woven of others' expectations is exhausting."
> *Bossy Bit #12*

— Eight —

Marvelous Mommy

If you judge people, you have no time to LOVE them.
Mother Teresa

I did not know **Marvelous Mommy** before she had children. She has two, both girls. One is a teenager and the other a toddler. The contrast between her experiences with each of her daughters could not have been more glaring.

Her first daughter profoundly shaped Marvelous Mommy's approach to mothering. She was a delight in every way. She came into the world with relative ease, and her arrival was celebrated by all. As Mommy tells the story, from the moment she first held her baby in her arms, her daughter looked back at her with pure love. She nursed easily, slept regularly, and grew into a cooperative, loving child. Mommy's heart burst with love for her daughter. She felt like she couldn't ever do enough for this miracle of a person.

Eleven years later, the conditions surrounding her second pregnancy were awful in almost every way. Though she was totally devoted to her first daughter, Mommy had always dreamed about having another child—just not at that moment. Mommy's life circumstances were such that adding another baby to her family was simply unthinkable. She was nearing forty and medically high-risk. She was unmarried and desperate to end an abusive relationship with the baby's father. There was no family nearby for support. She agonized over the dilemma and eventually decided to end the pregnancy.

The women at the abortion clinic were helpful and patient. They didn't allow rash decisions. Mommy wanted the procedure to be quick—over before she lost her conviction. She begged, but was given no choice. The clinic's policy was to wait another six weeks.

Mommy returned to the clinic, telling no one. Quiet tears rolled down her cheeks with each step towards the procedure. She always wanted another baby and at her age, this was certainly her last chance. She sat down with the Planned Parenthood doctor who saw her distress and placed her hand on Mommy's and asked, "Is this *really* what you want?" It wasn't. Mommy was in love with her baby and decided she would protect that

Marvelous Mommy

baby with everything in her, consequences be damned. She already knew that she was willing to sacrifice anything to hold this beautiful soul in her arms. The doctor hugged her and supported her decision wholeheartedly. Mommy left the office that day with not only a baby in her belly, but a conviction to thrive—together.

The rest of the pregnancy was a daily struggle, and it did not improve after delivery. Her life fell apart. It was worse than her worst nightmares. It seemed her baby was sensitive to the negative emotional energy. She cried all the time, and it was no normal cry. The hospital staff and the caregivers who helped with delivery said they'd never heard a baby sound like that. Any time Mommy held her, touched her, or tried to soothe her the baby would scream like her soul was being tortured. This tormented Mommy, creating what she describes as, "an anguished, uninterrupted ten-month feedback loop." She feared she would lose her sanity. She spent her days curled up, sleep-deprived, fingers in her ears, rocking her screaming baby, and crying at the pain and helplessness of it all.

Nobody knew what to do. Doctors diagnosed the problem as 'colic.' Nothing alleviated it. Mommy had known exactly what to do with her first daughter. Now, her powerlessness caused soul-wrenching grief and guilt. The badge of honor she had worn as a spectacular mother was now an emblem of shame as she utterly failed to soothe her suffering baby girl.

Fortunately for Mommy, that cycle finally ended, and the family's life improved. But giving her daughters all that they need still stresses Mommy. She is a single mother, who works full-time, with two very different children. Sometimes she is forced to rely on her older daughter's help. She hates that. Delegating her mothering responsibilities feels like an admission of failure.

I admire Mommy's dedication. She wants her daughters to feel loved, worthy, safe, and appreciated. Everyday living means constant compromise and disappointment. Her ideal life doesn't match the *reality* of her life. This keeps shame and guilt ever-present.

And that's how she teaches me about Grace. Bossy Grace is the non-judgmental acceptance of what is real in ourselves and others. Mommy just can't take that step. She believes she can control everything in her world and take care of everyone around her, and when she fails to deliver, as we all do sometimes, she is devastated and falls apart. She neglects many of her own needs while constantly measuring herself and others by their ability to 'do it all.'

We all wear multiple hats. Priorities are not stagnant. They come and go, shift and bend. We all have the same number of minutes in a day, but for Mommy to be her best self, she must find a way to care for herself. Marvelous Mommy is out of balance. She needs to find outlets to express her creative drives. Being the best parent she can be is not simply what she does for her kids, it's also modeling what it means to live an authentic life of purpose.

Marvelous Mommy allows me to see in her an example of what grace is not. Bossy Grace allows us to see the bigger picture and put priorities in their proper perspective. When we remember to manage our expectations, our stress levels remain in the healthy zone. As leaders, zero stress is unrealistic, but we do not want it to weigh on us, consume us, and ultimately cause illness. Bossy Grace helps us avoid that and creates balance between our dedication and our peace. It helps us remember that we are worthy and valuable and that it is our responsibility to cultivate our talents and put them at the service of others—our children, yes, but also all others we love and encounter.

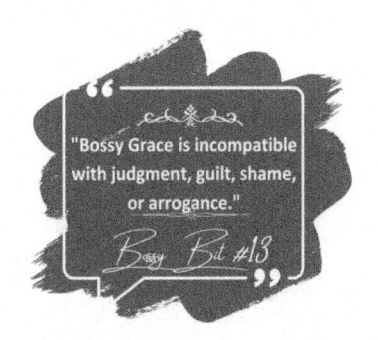

> "Bossy Grace is incompatible with judgment, guilt, shame, or arrogance."
>
> *Bossy Bit #13*

—Nine—
Amazing Ariel

The best way to find yourself is to lose yourself in the service of others.
Mahatma Gandhi

I call my fourth friend **Amazing Ariel** because she reminds me of the hero in *The Little Mermaid.* Just like that story's character, Ariel constantly seeks adventure and new experiences. She is happiest holding sea turtles or dancing on the beach in Bermuda. Ariel will throw caution to the wind if it means the chance to broaden her horizons or to experience more of life. Almost any risk seems worth it to her. *Amazing* is her favorite word, and *amazed* is her favorite state of being.

Ariel is also like the Disney princess in her approach to romantic love. She once told me about a time when she was living alone in a house in the woods. A tree fell through her roof. The basement flooded. The township considered condemning her home. She became a literal damsel in distress. Contractors told her there was nothing that could be done. Some friends knew of one person who might be able to help. He came reluctantly, only after she softened him with desperate pleas. He was not physically her type—long, gray hair, a bit rough around the edges. He was also strong, brave, and charismatic. His smile lit the room ... and Ariel's world.

In addition to the house crumbling around her, Ariel faced another calamity. Apparently, when the house was vacant, snakes moved in before she did. The first clue was when she removed a blender from a kitchen cupboard and what she thought was the cord in her hand, was actually an eight-foot snake. Her home had become a nightmare. Calls to 911 were the norm. These brushes happened so regularly the emergency dispatchers began to recognize her number and voice.

As this man restored her home to a livable condition, a snake crawled through the ceiling. At wits' end, with tears streaking down her face and her baby in her arms, she pleaded for him to get rid of the snake. He looked at her in disbelief, then jumped up, punched through the drop-tile, grabbed the snake, and asked her where she wanted him to put it. She looked up and saw a savior, a warrior, a man who could protect her, and would do anything for her. He was Superman, and he chose her.

Amazing Ariel

Sadly, their romance did not go the distance. The next five years were wonderful, yet she again found herself alone and desperate to regain those feelings of adoration and being chosen.

She believed she would never have such feelings again, but finally found her Prince Charming a few years later. Ariel in *The Little Mermaid* willingly gives up her voice for the sake of a man, her prince. In our Ariel's case, she did something similar. Her new prince catered to her every desire. He seemed to have a window into her inner world. He created the kind of experiences that were the answer to her lifelong dreams. This man checked every box Ariel wanted in her idealized image. He was gorgeous—physically chiseled, stylish, and capable in so many ways. They would own the dance floor—you know, like in movies when the stars would dance so amazingly that others circled around to watch. Ariel felt like she was dancing on air. He would sing to her at karaoke nights—and blow the crowd away with his performance. She felt like she had been chosen by the most desirable man in the world.

He supported her endeavors. He promoted her and helped her with her work. He showered her with incredibly thoughtful gifts. Once, he presented her with an end table he had made. On the marble top, he had laminated photos of special moments from her life. No gift could have pleased her more.

It wasn't just the physical gifts or whisking her away to exotic locales that charmed Ariel. This man constantly told her how beautiful she was, that she was the most desirable woman in the world. He made her feel like there could be no other woman for him. It was music to her ears.

Ariel was so swept away by the romance that she metaphorically gave up her voice. Other relationships and priorities took a back seat. She became uncharacteristically passive. The habits that had built her up and energized her physically and mentally went by the wayside. She indulged in the spontaneous. She took cues for her daily decisions from her prince.

But life wasn't constant fun. That's not reality, even for Ariel. She started noticing conflicting signs in things this man said and did. At first, she rationalized them away, thinking *He didn't really mean that,* or *He did the best he could with that. He'll learn to do better next time.* Her instincts were screaming, but she didn't listen. She had given up her voice, even the inner one.

Ariel had never before known a narcissistic sociopath. She could not believe it was possible for one person to go to such elaborate lengths to manipulate and control another. She was blind to the fact that someone could feel deep satisfaction from using others. She had not yet learned that in fairy tales, there is a Prince

Charming and there is a bad guy. But with a narcissist, Prince Charming IS the bad guy.

She had been the perfect target for this predator. Her innocent romanticism made her vulnerable to someone who would stop at nothing to fulfill her fantasies. And that is exactly what he did. She marveled at his ingenuity and boundless energy. When he used it to make her fantasies come true, he produced many of the peak experiences of her life. But he also used his remarkable abilities against her. She later discovered that he read her private journal to learn her deepest thoughts—her impressions, desires, and fears. He used that intelligence to manipulate her.

In the beginning, it was all 'love bombs,' the term used to describe outsized gestures made by narcissists to favorably pluck their target's heartstrings. When Ariel finally began to see that all was not as it seemed, she pulled away. That's when her Prince Charming transformed into the Prince of Darkness. He used her fears to keep her where he wanted her—dependent and under his total control.

When Ariel finally put her foot down and ended the relationship, he would not let it go. He verbally abused her. He harassed her. He stalked her. She didn't know that he had broken into a neighboring townhouse and cut holes through the firewalls to access her attic. He used the latest technology to track her and spy on her. He broke into her home and installed cameras—in the microwave, in the bathroom fan, even directly over her bed.

When he was arrested, he had buried himself in her backyard, wrapped in fabric, wearing a fake beard in the middle of the night at 23 degrees Fahrenheit. He saw everything she did in her bathroom and bedroom. He heard every conversation and recorded all of it to use against her. If you haven't experienced this kind of trauma, it can be difficult to comprehend. She remains unable to open her windows and has never recovered from the fear.

Though profoundly affected by this experience, Ariel has not abandoned her romantic nature and zest for life. She is too much about the here and now to lose hope or even really to change all that much. She wants to live in the magic of Oz. She sees routine and responsibility as the colorless, dreary world of Kansas. We laugh when I tell her she is still allowed to visit Oz, but she can't stay. That seems to help her manage the disappointment.

Ariel's type of love, while delightful in the moment, is also a consuming, self-centered, and sometimes destructive love. Desire and indulgence are shallow. Bossy Love is not a feeling—romantic or otherwise. It is a decision and an action. Bossy Love is the sacrifice of the expedient for the important. Sometimes it's okay to indulge our impulses, but making indulgence a habit does not lead to happily-ever-after. My friend Ariel does not

Amazing Ariel

realize love isn't about what you want. It's about what you (and others around you) *need*.

So many of us think of love as a feeling that overtakes us. We believe we will be swept away by a love so encompassing it becomes undeniable. And while I hope you have the opportunity to experience such moments, I don't consider that real love. It's certainly not Bossy Love.

Our relationships and even our families can fall apart when we rely upon others to fulfill our desires. We wait for love to fill our cup. I am grateful Ariel has let me learn about her version of love, because on the surface it looks like the love of fairy tales. Upon closer inspection, however, Ariel consistently teaches me everything about what love is NOT.

"Bossy Love sucks!"

Bossy Bit #14

Part THREE

—Ten—

The Real Bossy Girl

There's something special about a woman who dominates in a man's world. It takes a certain grace, strength, intelligence, fearlessness, and the nerve to never take no for an answer.
Rihanna

Just like Weslyn, Pearl, Mommy, and Ariel, we are all meant to walk our path for a reason and a purpose. Every trial makes us exactly who we are. A deep look in the mirror can be difficult. It was for me. Mine resulted in the discovery of my four friends. Yes, you guessed it. Weslyn, Pearl, Mommy, and Ariel are pieces of the same person: *Me*. They personify my harshest trials and greatest joys.

Every story I told you is true. I am; in fact, blessed with two beautiful daughters, Kianna and Korinna. I live for them. They are the most incredible girls I could ever have dreamed of—both of them. I never quit so that I can be an example for them to live out their purpose boldly, without inhibition. I pray they will courageously embody love in action. The relationships and family dynamics I shared are also true. My mother has been a model of grace and love her entire life, and my dad is and forever will be my hero and my logical sounding board.

Concerning their physical appearances, when each friend takes their turn at the wheel, it surprises me how much my appearance shifts in the direction of their self-image. My internal emotional landscape resembles each woman when they are 'driving.' Now that I'm coming to know them, I can recognize which one is behind the wheel. And as I worked through this process of self-discovery, the highlights and lowlights of my life revealed themes (and I suspect yours will, too!) that shockingly fell in line with the principles I had already defined as the Bossy Values.

> "Only by embracing the truest versions of ourselves can we discover and accomplish our purpose."
>
> Bossy Bit #15

My friends became more substantial as I discovered them, named them, and paid attention to them. Like anybody, they need to be known, recognized, and valued; they need to be *seen*. When I give them this gift, I act as a better friend to them. They, in turn, become better friends to me, to each other, and even to people who don't live inside my head.

My friends can be self-centered, inconsiderate, and bull-headed. Although they all co-exist within me, they do not see eye-to-eye. It's very similar to a team or an organization. We strive to create balance by bringing together complementary strengths and weaknesses. When each team player focuses on their own desires, they fail to achieve the mission and mutual respect. There's a similar dynamic with the friends we'll learn to love through this process. They can be taught how to share, follow, and support one another's greatness, but they are not naturally empathic—just like the rest of us.

As I got to know my friends, I came to another realization: They exist to protect me, but protection is a double-edged sword of which we must be wary. Barriers protect us from harm, but they also protect us from connection and curiosity. If we don't stay keenly aware, our barriers become prison walls that abolish our freedom and our power. As we learn to love our friends and reduce fear of the outside world, we embrace and yield our power appropriately.

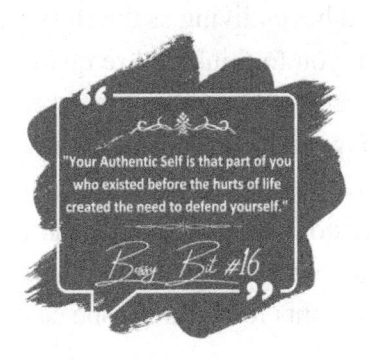

> "Your Authentic Self is that part of you who existed before the hurts of life created the need to defend yourself."
>
> Bossy Bit #16

As I winnowed the friends, the wounding, and the trauma from my authentic self, I realized that ownership of my power was suddenly available to me. I had nothing left to prove. I had no reason to hide. I could celebrate the victories of the women around me with pure joy and admiration. I could give the love that others need without depleting myself. Imagine what the world would look like if all women could live this pure, vulnerable, authentic life!

I now know who the Bossy Girl REALLY is. She is ambitious and unapologetic for it. She wants to contribute to the world in a big way. She wants to help as many people as she possibly can, and then some. She is a communicator and a leader. Her willpower makes her a formidable adversary, and she is comfortable being in charge. Her team will get things done and they will be better people because of her leadership.

Please know that there's a caveat. Identifying your authentic self and owning your power is beautiful, but it isn't easy. I'm sure you can imagine that there will be headwinds, scrutiny, and criticism. No matter how strong you are, it is difficult. As I came back to life after my traumatic brain injury and began living as the Bossy Girl, I heard it all. "Who are you to think you're qualified to lead a women's movement?" or "What a joke, you're going to redefine a word?" On top of it, my friends, those partial parts of me and previous coping mechanisms, want nothing to do with it. Weslyn doesn't want to be on stage, *any* stage. Pearl fears the risk of such a big mission; she only wants to do things she can do perfectly. Mommy resents any time and energy diverted from her children. Ariel fears that the responsibilities, commitments, and burdens that accompany mission completion will take time away from enjoying all that life can offer.

If we decide to own all of our power, our resolve must be stronger than our doubt and our naysayers. Together, we will get to know the authentic part of you that is analogous to my Bossy Girl. You will learn to nourish her and empower yourself and your voice. We will find the conviction to never play small or accept less than you deserve.

Let's go change the world in ways that only YOU can!

"Your full power comes when you decide who takes the wheel."

Bossy Bit #17

― Eleven ―

The Friends Model

*I do not wish for women to have power over men;
but over themselves.*
Mary Wollstonecraft

Now it's your turn to use the Friends Model. It's a big ask that I don't take lightly. This will take time. You may shed some tears. You will examine aspects of yourself you have not thought about—or maybe deliberately avoided—for years. We will rip apart stories that you've told yourself to cover up past pain and injuries. The process may be disturbing, upsetting, and possibly even traumatic. Do it anyway. It will be worth it.

You are currently standing at an inflection point on the Yellow Brick Road. We are making tangible, lasting, important, and positive changes. It's time to make an iron-clad, irrevocable decision to seek the wizard, together. We will systematically remove the obstacles—both internal and external—that get in our way.

The personal benefits of this work are nearly immeasurable. Using the Beautifully Bossy Leadership Model and the Friends Model will not only make you a more effective leader, but it will also help you live more elegantly. You will have a greater sense of purpose that will connect you to the missions that matter; and more importantly, you will help those around you to do the same.

If we are to effectively serve others, we must start with a long, hard look in the mirror. This image will vividly reflect the starting line of the Yellow Brick Road. One journey may be longer than another, but all of them can be treacherous. It's important to note that I am not a psychologist, and this is not therapy. I am a leadership development consultant and training facilitator who knows what works and what doesn't when it comes to motivating individuals and teams to take effective action and achieve a mission. While there are many leadership styles, there are universal principles the most potent leaders embody. I am here to make you successful.

> "Only by embracing the truest versions of ourselves can we discover and accomplish our purpose."
>
> *Bossy Bit #15*

— Twelve —

Who Teaches You Courage?

There is a hidden blessing in the most traumatic things we go through in our lives. My brain always goes to, 'Where is the hidden blessing? What is my gift?'
Sara Blakely

For better or for worse, I have had many experiences that caused my friend, Wounded Weslyn, to emerge. It probably began with the treatment I received as a young girl from both of my grandmothers. As it turned out, it might have been for the best, because at age fifteen, Weslyn saved my life.

On the beach at our family vacation spot, I was the victim of a brutal knifepoint rape by two older men. I didn't talk about it with anyone—not my parents, the police, my friends—no one. When my mother saw the bruises and the psychic wounds I couldn't hide, I told her I had been in a fight and didn't want to talk about it.

It was a mighty blow to my sense of self. Perfect Pearl, who dominated that stage of my life, was utterly devastated. She did everything 'right.' Her life had to be perfect. For her, life was over; she could never be perfect again. I found myself on the edge of a dock, about to throw myself into the dark ocean and bring my suffering to a quick end.

Weslyn grabbed the wheel. She took the pain and suffering on herself. That's what she was born to do. It's her purpose. When we returned from vacation, to shelter me from the mental suffering that accompanies this kind of trauma, Weslyn remained in the driver's seat. Vulnerable and hurting, Weslyn projected the opposite image. Her style choices felt edgy and intimidating. I cut my long blond hair and dyed it black. My style and appearance went aggressive and dark. I lifted weights and got strong, stronger than most of the guys I knew.

When Weslyn drives, she puts up as many barriers as she can. She avoids vulnerability at all costs. She has serious control issues that come from repeated trauma. Maybe you can relate. Most women have found themselves feeling unsafe at one time or another. We feel victimized, or we live with the fear of becoming a victim.

Weslyn is dedicated to keeping me from feeling scared. Like a soldier who has seen combat, she's been hardened. One of the ways I can tell that Weslyn has the wheel is weight gain. She wants to be big. To her, mass equals safety. Since I started using the Friends Model to recognize her, I have a new habit. When I feel her, I look into the mirror and talk to her. I tell her she is okay, safe, beautiful, worthy, and loved.

I am thankful for all that Weslyn has done for me. Of my friends, she is the one who is closest to my heart. Weslyn never models courage because she will not act in the face of fear, but she allows me to be courageous, serving as my safety net when I get hurt while taking risks.

Maybe you have a friend like Wounded Weslyn, or maybe the friend who teaches you courage is nothing like her. Maybe you feel your authentic self is courageous by nature, or maybe not. We all face fears, and we all benefit from knowing and developing the parts of ourselves that respond to those fears. Remember that courage is NOT the absence of fear. In fact, when we are fearless, courage cannot exist. Only in the face of fear can we practice courage. Bossy Courage is being afraid and doing the right thing anyway. It's the key that unlocks our potential.

Who Teaches You Courage?
A Workbook

Now that you are squarely on the Yellow Brick Road it's time to unlock whatever chains may be holding you back from your full potential. We'll start by connecting you to the friend who teaches you courage. (Remember, this friend teaches you courage by showing you what it is not.) My answers to these questions are included not to sway you, but merely to encourage you and maybe inspire your own effective answers.

1) Think of at least three times when you were hurt, lost, vulnerable, or defeated. Think about how you felt. Write down your thoughts and feelings.

A)_____
_____
_____

B)_____
_____
_____

C)_____
_____
_____

Bossy Girl's answers:

A) 2016: Traumatic Brain injury from auto accident. Retreated. Hid. Didn't want people to know. Became needy. I wanted my mom. VERY lonely.

B) 2020: Business falling apart because of pandemic, complicated by medical and personal issues. Powerless, feared failure and dependency.

C) 2019: Attack of narcissistic sociopath. Challenges with extremely sensitive infant. Isolation. Shouldering financial disaster. No sleep. Health issues. All at the same time.

Did you come up with at least three answers? If not, another possibility is to remember the times when you were most afraid. What happened? What did you eventually do? How did you feel when you took action? Did that produce any long-lasting changes? Write your answers in the spaces above.

2) Look at your answers. Are there similarities between the experiences? Is there a common weakness, vulnerability, or blind spot in two or more of the events? Does it seem like you are a victim? If so, of what? Write your answers:

_____
_____
_____

Bossy Girl's answer: *The similarity is that I felt powerless and vulnerable. I most feared not being successful. Not succeeding in my mission would create suffering for those who depend on me, especially my daughters.*

3) Write three adjectives to describe how these similarities make you feel:

　　A) _____

　　B) _____

　　C) _____

Bossy Girl's answers: *Wounded, Powerless, Fearful.*

4) If these feelings and these adjectives defined an entire person, what would they want most?

_____
_____
_____

Bossy Girl's answer: *She wants to be safe. She wants the pain to stop. She wants to feel like she can't be hurt.*

5) What does she fear most?

_____
_____
_____

Bossy Girl's answer: *Destruction and the choices of those around her that expose her to risk, danger, and vulnerability.*

6) What is her response to pain and fear?

_____
_____
_____

Bossy Girl's answer: *She hides. She puts up defenses. She pushes people away, but she doesn't want to be alone.*

7) I want you to see her as a person. She might look like you, but there are differences. What are they?

_____
_____
_____

Bossy Girl's answer: *She's big and imposing. She has worried, sad eyes that show her defeat. She doesn't say much. She's rugged and ragged.*

8) What is her defining characteristic? Choose one word:

_____

Bossy Girl's answer: *Wounded.*

9) Final step, for now: What is her name?

_____

Bossy Girl's answer: *Weslyn. The name in German means "defending warrior." She steps up to take the hits for me.*

Meet your friend _____. I'm thrilled for you to get to know them. He or she teaches you about *Courage*. Remember, courage is our ability to defeat fear's debilitating effects and do the right thing anyway. If your friend is anything like Weslyn, her first instinct is to hide from trouble. Her impulses are a function of environment and life circumstances—a collaborative creation between you and the other people who have been significant in your life.

As I said, Weslyn is my favorite friend. Without her I would not be here. She has proven to be a major source of strength for me. She is my rock. She suffers. She has proven, time and time again, that she can take it. She is the one who allows me to live authentically—to speak truthfully, even when it hurts. She takes the pain and leaves room in my heart to love other people. I hope your new friend does the same things for you. As you increase your capacity for Bossy Courage, you speed your path toward becoming the Beautifully Bossy leader you are meant to be.

— Thirteen —

Who Teaches You Authenticity?

*The privilege of the lifetime is to become
who you truly are.*
Carl Jung

Perfect Pearl was born from a need for perfection that was not defined by what was inside, but by her aversion to any kind of shame, ridicule, or embarrassment. She walks through life knowing that if she exceeds every expectation and never falters, she will gain acceptance and popularity. As far as I can tell, Pearl died when I was hit by that truck. Any illusion of perfection was destroyed by my inability to read, my food stamp card, my pathetic lack of balance, and my propensity to fall on my face (literally and figuratively). Embarrassment went by the wayside, replaced with immense gratitude and sheer determination.

Today, I shine in the glory of being perfectly imperfect. Since my brain injury, I have yet to deliver one perfect session. I am reminded of one of my first keynote speeches since the pandemic. As I prepared, I felt the weight of the world on my shoulders. Although I had been facilitating classroom leadership sessions regularly, I hadn't been on the "big stage" since before the injury. I invested entire days creating the perfect PowerPoint presentation and carefully curated notes. I even practiced the session in advance—a very uncommon occurrence.

The day of the session, I walked onto the main ballroom stage of my very own alma mater. There were at least a thousand seats, including balcony seating, a projection screen that dwarfed those at rock concerts, and news anchors on each side of me. The spotlights shone so brightly that I couldn't make out the faces in the audience, but off I went. The speech began without a hitch, but approximately twenty minutes in . . . I went blank. I had no idea what I was talking about or why. It was like that nightmare you see in the movies when you're suddenly standing before the audience, naked, with everyone just staring, waiting to see what you will do next.

I had an opportunity before me. I could call Pearl to drive, or I could get real and authentic about who I really was and just strive to be the best version of me. I chose option two. I giggled and said to the audience, "Brain injuries are real, folks." I felt people soften and the tension ease. I grabbed my notes, took a peek, jumped right back in, and gave one of the most impactful speeches of my career. My love and acceptance of vulnerability provided each participant an opportunity to love the imperfections in themselves. That day we were present in the ring together fighting to become the truest versions of ourselves.

What is the truest version of you? Who are you? What were you meant for? Have you ever felt like you spent so much time surrounding yourself with the thoughts and judgments of others that you no longer even know what it was that you were passionate about? You were so immersed in What would so-and-so think? that you no longer knew what you thought. Perfect Pearl was born to protect me, and your Perfect Pearl was born to protect you. The problem is that she was forged out of what is wrong in our world—those experiences that hurt us. She was formed in response to the expectations that have been placed upon us. She is a barrier between you and true connection with others.

Finding our authentic selves requires investing time and energy in getting and being quiet. I spent six months in a dark room with only my thoughts. It was the worst time of my life and I hope that is never required of you. You don't need that experience to find yourself, but I used that time to ask questions like:

- What am I truly grateful for?
- What am I passionate about?

- What brings out the delicious joy and celebration of my spirit?
- What am I good at?
- What am I doing because I want to please others, but should have said no?
- What brought me joy as a child?

Mark Twain said that the two most important days of your life are the day you were born and the day you find out why. As we live out the authentic fingerprint we were given, we will uncover the reason why—our purpose. It awaits. Today you become the author of your choices. You get to decide what kind of leader you want to be.

> "Only through vulnerability can we uncover our purpose and the truest version of ourself."
>
> *Bossy Bit #19*

The questions below will help you discern and define the friend who teaches you Authenticity. Remember, our friends mostly teach us the Bossy Values by showing us what they are NOT. I offer my answers not to influence you or to steer you away from what rings true for you, but rather to help you if your answers don't come easily.

Who Teaches You Authenticity?
A Workbook

1) List or circle the roles you had around age 10. Examples: Daughter, Sister, Granddaughter, Victim, Achiever, Athlete, Student, Supporter.

_____
_____
_____

Bossy Girl's answers: *Daughter, Sister, Granddaughter, Achiever, Student.*

2) Pick the role that had the deepest, longest-lasting effect on you. To what degree and in what ways does it affect you today?

_____
_____
_____

Bossy Girl's answer: *Daughter. I want to make my parents proud.*

3) What were the expectations of others as they related to that role?

_____
_____
_____

Bossy Girl's answer: *None. I couldn't have asked for more love and acceptance. My parents always told me I was special. Unintentionally, they put me on a quest to figure out what they meant by that.*

4) Going back to the initial roles you circled, how would those involved in that relationship describe you?

Role   Description

_____   _____
_____   _____
_____   _____
_____   _____

Bossy Girl's answers:

Daughter: *My parents told me I was special, strong, and capable of whatever I put my mind to.*

Granddaughter: *My grandparents saw me as not enough—not religious enough, thin enough, etc.*

Sister: *I was the one who didn't get in trouble. The golden child who got the breaks.*

Achiever: *National Honor Society, cheer captain, student council, teacher's pet.*

5) If others had chosen your occupation for you, what would it be? Is that the path you took? If not, why not?

_____
_____
_____

Who Teaches You Authenticity?

Bossy Girl's answer: *Audiologist. Kind of. My dad had a Miracle-Ear franchise and wanted me to take over. I went to school for it and hated it. There was no joy or sense of calling. As soon as I changed my major, he sold the businesses. I often looked back with regret. I probably would have made a lot of money. But, in the end, it just wasn't my purpose. And living your purpose is priceless.*

6) Look at your answers. Are there consistencies or themes? Write down your thoughts about them.

_____

_____

_____

Bossy Girl's answer: *The ways that I have been viewed all seem intense and polarizing. People either loved me or hated me. There was never any gray area.*

7) Now imagine if the history you described had happened to another person. How would you describe that person?

_____

_____

_____

Bossy Girl's answer: *She's always doing the right thing, but she's not so much the people-pleaser it might sound like she is. She makes her decisions through the lens of achievement and being 'right.' She's afraid to get into trouble. She lives her life as though everything she does is in full view of everyone else—whether they would have done the same or not, she wants them to think her behavior was good and admirable. She's outspoken, maybe even pushy.*

8) Let's keep imagining her as another person. Maybe she looks like you. But if she could change her physical appearance, what would those changes be? In her mind, what does she look like?

_____

_____

_____

Bossy Girl's answer: *She's polished. She's always put together. Her nails match her purse. She's usually overdressed. She's mature beyond her years. She has the look of an accomplished person.*

9) What does she want most? What does she want least?

Bossy Girl's answer:
Most: *She wants to make people proud of her. She wants to always do the right thing. She wants to stand up for what is right. No flaws.*

Least: *She doesn't want to be unmasked, revealed, or seen as anything other than perfect (imposter syndrome).*

10) What is her defining characteristic? Choose one word:

_____

Bossy Girl's answer: *Perfect.*

11) Final step, for now: What is her name?

_____

Bossy Girl's answer: *I picked Pearl because it's a beautiful gem that is formed in a dark, yucky place. I consider Pearl beautiful. She is high-strung and perfectionistic perhaps, but her beauty is in her ambition, and she will do the right thing, whatever that might mean, and no matter how hard it is.*

Meet your friend _____. I'm thrilled for you to get to know her/him/them. She teaches you about Authenticity. If your friend is anything like Pearl, she doesn't want to show any flaws. When Pearl is at the wheel, it's hard for me to be vulnerable and graceful—especially to myself. Your friend's impulses come from your Authentic Self, but they are not perfectly aligned. She is there to protect you from rejection. When you're a Beautifully Bossy Leader, her services will no longer be needed.

For the longest time, I thought I WAS Pearl. I am thankful to her for the standards she has set and the achievements she has driven me to obtain. But she is not me. Now that I know Pearl, my purpose is even clearer. I hope the same is true for you as you get to know your new friend.

— Fourteen —

Who Teaches You Grace?

Remember, you have been criticizing yourself for years and it hasn't worked. Try approving of yourself and see what happens.
Louise Hay

Marvelous Mommy sprang to life when my eldest daughter was born. The moment Kianna was placed in my arms, nothing else mattered. I was ready for her arrival—married to my best friend and secure. Her disposition, behavior, and habits were all a parent could possibly hope for in a child. Eleven years later, Korinna was born, and the two experiences were like night and day.

Korinna was meant to be. She was a miracle. According to the doctors, endometriosis had pulled my ovary and fallopian tube so far apart that an egg should not have been able to traverse the space. At the time, though, *miracle* wasn't the word I would have used. Her biological father was a very real danger. As intended, this baby would forever cement me to him. To escape him, I decided to terminate the pregnancy.

Marvelous Mommy simply would not have it. In the parking lot of the abortion clinic the day of the scheduled procedure, Mommy rose up and grabbed the wheel. Literally. We drove away, and in so doing she saved Korinna's life. It was a conscious decision—my life in exchange for my baby's.

That is exactly what happened as I fought for my life against excruciating physical maladies, built a leadership development business, suffered isolation from my parents (my support structure) during the pandemic, and narrowly escaped death at the hands of a demented, determined criminal. All of those trials were amplified by Korinna's extraordinary sensitivity to any negative energies within me or our household.

Though I made drastic changes in how I approached my business (and everything else), it was impossible for me to give my girls everything they needed and deserved. Whenever I failed in that regard, I felt soul-crushing guilt. If you are or ever have been a single mom, you likely know exactly what I'm talking about. I can't change my baby girl's biology. What I can do is consistently assure her she is deeply worthy of love and belonging. Every single day I am gifted with her presence and infectious joy. I will always show Korinna how much I love her and want her. She is the most beautiful blessing.

It wasn't planned this way, but it's probably not a coincidence that of my four friends, Marvelous Mommy does not have a proper name of her own. She is totally defined by her role. Sometimes, I must tell Mommy to sit down and be quiet. She is so fierce and determined to love her daughters that she has no time or sensitivity to other priorities. The girls always come first, but in real life, they are not the ONLY priority. Here's a recent example:

I had scheduled an important video conference. To make the call, I had to pick up Korinna early from daycare. My normal rule is that my office is off limits—it is my sanctuary where I can be Bossy without distraction. But on this day, I had no choice; I had to have Korinna with me as Kianna was not home to help. There were over a hundred high-performing professionals from all over the world on the call, and I had been selected, without prior notice, to speak to the group. Disheveled, baby crawling on me and wanting my attention, I spoke about the Worldwide Women's Wholeness Wave. The Bossy Girl, and Perfect Pearl, were mortified. This was not the image they would have chosen. Marvelous Mommy was a pain in my butt, too. She didn't want me on the call; she kept wanting me to hang up and attend to Korinna. I finished the call.

Then I braced myself for the horrible feedback of my sub-par performance, but what I received blew me away. People did not see the mess about which I had been so self-conscious. They saw a woman committed to both her daughter and the mission of making the world a better place. They saw a mother willing to model the behavior she thought best—being Bossy, and they responded with offers of podcast interviews and notes of appreciation.

I almost can't find the words to tell you how it feels when grace is truly present. When you are forgiven, without judgment, it relieves the pressure of perfection. When we give grace to ourselves and others, we alleviate the fear of failure and create space for courage and authenticity. When we hold graceful space, we create meaningful connections based on the truest versions of ourselves.

> "The illusion of control impedes Grace."
> Bossy Bit #20

If you are a mother, you may identify with Marvelous Mommy. Feel free to use her name! If not, don't worry. You have a friend who can help you manifest more grace. She may be overly dedicated to a cause at the expense of other parts of your life. When you answer the questions below, try to connect to that part of you.

Who Teaches You Grace?
A Workbook

Identify the part of yourself that is hard on you and maybe others as well. She may have unrealistic standards and expectations about a role you play in life. She may have control issues. Keep these in mind as you form your responses.

1) When were you most critical of yourself or disappointed the people, you love?

A)_____
_____
_____

B)_____
_____
_____

C)_____
_____
_____

Bossy Girl's answers:
A) Failed relationships. I've failed myself, my daughters, my parents, even my career.

B) Not understanding how to best parent my second daughter—feeling lost and helpless.

C) Plight of a single mom trying to make up for her children having the disadvantage of a broken family.

2) Read over your responses but do it from a different perspective. Pretend you're reading the observations of somebody else you love and respect who only wants the best for you. What would they say to you?

A)_____

B)_____

C)_____

Bossy Girl's answers:
A) You did the best you could with the information you had. Failure is never permanent. Every season has meaning.

B) What have you done well? What are the good moments? How can you create more of that? How can you take a break? You are fifty percent of the equation.

C) What are the moments only possible because you are the mother you are? Tell me what you love about your kids. Would you rather have your children in a healthy family with you alone, or in a toxic, destructive family with both parents? Even though your children might not have everything you want them to, do you embody the example you would want them to follow?

3) If there was something this person wanted to focus on completely, what would it be? How does this influence their behavior?

___

Bossy Girl's answer: *She wants to be the BEST mom. The way she evaluates herself in this way is dual. She asks: "What's possible?" and "How do I exceed expectations and what others might do in that situation?" She makes it difficult to feel accomplished when she does that.*

4) What's in her way?

___

Bossy Girl's answer: *Bossy Girl's mission. Ariel's desires. Weslyn's fear.*

5) She looks like you. But if she could change her physical appearance, what would those changes be? In her mind, what does she look like?

_____
_____
_____

Bossy Girl's answer: *Ponytail. Blends in. Brown hair. Soccer mom in a matching sweatsuit. Appearance irrelevant as long as she is not embarrassing to her children. She's tired, mascara under her eyes.*

6) What is her defining characteristic? Choose one word:

_____

Bossy Girl's answer: *Marvelous. That's how she must be seen by the world.*

7) Final step, for now: What is her name?

_____

Bossy Girl's answer: *Mommy. It's the only role she cares about.*

Meet your friend _____. I'm thrilled for you to get to know her/him/them. She teaches you about Grace. If your friend is anything like Marvelous Mommy, she's hard on you—unforgiving. She does not admit to human shortcomings. When Mommy is at the wheel, it's hard for me to be graceful, especially to myself. I am not saying we should excuse negligence, but shortcomings are real. We must acknowledge what is true. Whatever the situation, we have more Bossy Grace when we accept truth and go from there. This friend does not want to do that. Now that you know her, when you are not feeling particularly graceful, you can lovingly ask her to relinquish the wheel. It will be okay. By giving grace and eliminating judgment, we lead ourselves before leading others.

— Fifteen —
Who Teaches You Bossy Love?

Fight for the things you care about, but do it in a way that will lead others to join you.
Ruth Bader Ginsburg

You might not immediately relate to my Amazing Ariel. You may not even think you have a friend anything like her. But you do. This friend is the embodiment of the freedom to experience the things you want most—your passion. The business of life sometimes distracts us from noticing, but we all want something.

I admit it's a little bit silly for me to model a part of myself after a Disney Princess, but as I've gone through the work of creating the Friends Model, it makes more sense why she is who she is. Most of Disney's animated movies are retellings of timeless tales. They are timeless because they are universally true on a deep psychological level. They speak in archetypes that address some of life's most basic questions: Who am I? Do I matter? If so, why? If not, does anything matter? What am I capable of? What is good? What is evil? What is best? Stories give us tried-and-true templates so we don't need to start from scratch as we ponder these questions. They help us by preserving and sharing history's accumulated wisdom.

Ariel brings zest to my life unlike any of my other friends. Fully free and empowered, she wears flowing gowns that swirl in the air as she moves like Ginger Rogers across the dance floor. She connects me to some of the best experiences life has to offer. I love it when she takes the wheel.

As I have learned to acknowledge and appreciate Ariel, I have come to see how my childhood perceptions and desires shaped her. Ariel is bougie, all flash and bling. Growing up on a small farm, I dreamed of another world, just like Dorothy in Kansas dreaming of Oz. I even pestered my mom for sparkly shoes! She said they weren't practical. I wore makeup to school in the third grade. I wanted to go out to extravagant restaurants, but we didn't do that—my parents grew our food.

We lived in Hershey, Pennsylvania. I remember driving past the beautiful grounds of the Hotel Hershey, perched atop a hill, ensconced in lush greenery. It overlooked Hersheypark in the town fittingly called the

Who Teaches You Bossy Love?

Sweetest Place on Earth. I dreamed that someday I would be able to go to that place—eat at the fancy restaurants, enjoy the sumptuous spa, and stay in the luxurious rooms. As this memory came to me, I looked around my house and realized that I had subconsciously decorated it in the same style as the Hotel Hershey. That's the place Ariel wants to live.

She still wants to live outside of the norm, and the further away the better. That's why she likes to scuba dive and ride scooters along the New England coastline. Above all else, she does not want to be stuck or feel like she's missing out. She wants to experience the finer things. She wants to live in Oz.

Oz is a place of magical colors. It's vibrant and full of passion, but it also has wicked witches and flying monkeys. It's not for everybody. Really, it's best to live in both Kansas and Oz. Balance in all things, right? Without Ariel, I'm not sure I'd be able to visit Oz very often, and I really like it there.

Ariel's tendency to live in the moment and seek peak experiences has obviously brought me trouble. But that's okay. She has also traveled the world and done it all! She attracts people with her smile and infectious joy. She is backstage at concerts. She is hosting high-school reunions. She gets on stage in front of thousands and when she speaks, she helps others connect with true joy. For all of that, I'm thankful beyond words.

How about you? If you had to describe where your life is right now, would you say you're mostly in Kansas or in Oz? If both, how much of each? Is that working for you? Is that what you want?

Here's another pertinent question: What does any of this have to do with courageous love in action, or Bossy Love?

We're not typically born with the inclination for servant leadership. Think of the behavior of children. They are in a constant state of want. They're not very good at delaying gratification. They don't naturally sacrifice. Servant leadership puts the *needs of others* before your own *desires*. Ariel doesn't understand that in order to lead well she must put the mission first, people second, and herself last. In Ariel's world, she will always be first.

There are parts of us that are still two years old, and they don't disappear with time. They just get papered over. These are the parts of us that want what they want. For Ariel, this is how she gets in the way of Bossy Love. Not that the youthful *joie de vivre* she gives me is a bad thing. It is one of the superpowers I get from my friends. It works the same way for you.

I honor Ariel by letting her have her say. I have allowed her to decorate my home. I give her peak experiences when I can. She rewards me with dreams, lightness, optimism, and passion.

All of that is wonderful, but Ariel is *only* about the now. She neglects the future. Our future selves need and deserve respect and consideration. Our future selves benefit from sacrifice, planning, and delayed gratification. If we are practicing Bossy Love, we use discretion, discipline, and moderation to ensure that greed, gluttony, and pride do not get in our way. The process of exercise may not be fun, but the long-term benefits of a healthy body are never-ending. Saving money may feel like a drag, but financial preparedness will give you soul-soothing sleep. Our families, communities, friends, and our very own futures will benefit from Bossy Love in action.

Who Teaches You Bossy Love?
A Workbook

1) In your formative years, maybe as a young teen, what experiences did you dream of?

_____
_____
_____

Bossy Girl's answer: *I wanted to be fancy. I wanted to dress up in expensive, flowing, sparkly gowns. I wanted elegance. I wanted to dance at ritzy occasions. I wanted to ride horses on the beach. I wanted to go to exotic locations. I wanted to be wanted by an amazing man.*

2) If you had no restrictions, what would real-life Oz look like?

_____
_____
_____

Bossy Girl's answer: *It would be a transportation out of the norm. Something special, adventurous, romantic, and spontaneous. It would be a surprise.*

3) What are your greatest indulgences?

_____
_____
_____

Who Teaches You Bossy Love?

Bossy Girl's answer: *Dark chocolate! Good food of any kind. Romance. Dressing up. Time at the beach.*

4) Describe the above in detail. What does it look like? Where are you? What are you wearing? What do you see? Hear? Smell? Taste? Touch?

_____

_____

_____

Bossy Girl's answer: *I imagine a day at the beach. Not just any beach, but one where me and my special someone are the only people in sight. I look my best, rocking toned abs and the cutest bikini. I feel the sun's rays on my skin. They warm my body and my soul. I smell the coconut in the suntan lotion. The sky is deep blue, the day warm enough to make the gentle breeze welcome. I feel the strength in my lover's arms when he holds me, the humbling force of the surf, the power of my shiny-coated horse, the roughness of the sand, and the comforting softness of the fabric in my sheer cover-up and plush towel.*

5) Now read over your answers. What patterns or themes do you see?

_____

_____

_____

Bossy Girl's answer: *Princess, Fancy, Special, Adventure, Sunshine.*

6) If you had to sum that up with one word, what word would you use?

_____

Bossy Girl's answer: *Amazing*.

7) What's her first name?

_____

Bossy Girl's answer: *Ariel*.

Meet your friend _____. I'm thrilled for you to get to know her/him/them. She teaches you about Bossy Love. If your friend is anything like Ariel, she's a major source of your passion. Passion gives you energy. In this way, she contributes to your purpose and deserves your love. It may be true that you have denied her too frequently. That gives you a growth opportunity. The opposite may also be true. Left to her own devices, she can take us off track. And we pay a price when that happens.

This friend shows you what Bossy Love is not: an exclusive focus on your own emotions and experience. Bossy Love requires sacrifice and selflessness—traits that do not describe this friend. When you lead, it's important that you recognize this friend and take the wheel from her. Leadership is NOT about you!

— Sixteen —
Integrating Your Authentic Self

Impossible is not a fact. It's an opinion.
Laila Ali

I will never forget the day. I call it 'The Thursday.' After identifying my four friends and experiencing revelation after revelation, I was overwhelmed. I realized all of the trauma and challenge served something bigger than myself—my purpose! That thought sparked strong emotions. I was flooded with a soul-deep sense of gratitude. Then I was humbled by another thought: I had been appointed for this task. I felt I had endured, and continue to endure, so I may better serve my purpose: to help you, and ultimately all women, claim as much of your personal power as you can. That reframing changed everything. I was left with a profound sense of calm and well-being that I hadn't experienced in a long, long time.

Then something happened that I would never have expected in a million years.

This intense release of emotion gave way to a new way of being. I learned to love my friends, my enemies, the hurt, the fear, and the failure. I explored the existence of my friends and treated them as I would my own children. The depth of my love for them was the comfort needed for true freedom. I took a breath and, in an instant, my friends were gone!!! I mean, really gone. Not like they had merely let go of the wheel and snoozed in the back seat, but like they ceased to exist. It was an unexpected result that I am still working to understand. Suddenly, as I work to finish this book, I'm working to remember how my friends behaved instead of feeling as if they are still living in my skin.

After 'The Thursday,' everything changed. I have been forced to cope with life in new ways. Remember, our friends protect us. Without their presence, I'm left defenseless in stressful moments. I've had to learn to function only as my authentic self. It's strange and new. It's scary and raw. I am unpracticed in these responses. And it shows.

I have every confidence it will turn out for the better. I am learning. I also know that new friends may emerge, so I must be particularly careful. Yet, armed with the knowledge refined through this journey, and connected

Integrating Your Authentic Self

to my community, I feel the road I am on leads to a bright and exciting destination.

I want your future to shine like the sun. I don't know exactly how the identification of your friends will impact you, but they will give you more of your personal power. *That* I know. You may, sooner or later, experience something like 'The Thursday.' Maybe you won't. We all have different walks through this world. But I want you to know something: Authenticity is a choice you make every day. It is continuous. It never stops. That daily choice becomes a central part of your journey as a Beautifully Bossy leader.

> "Authenticity is a never-ending choice."
> *Bossy Bit #21*

Your style may be similar to mine, or it may be vastly different. I was born to throw down a gauntlet, to challenge people. I want to challenge your judgments about yourself because our judgments become a prison. The prison walls can grow so thick, you must kick out a brick just to get a peek at Oz awaiting outside. Look—it's all waiting for you! It's worth it. You might get scraped and bruised, but stay focused on the magic of Oz, on living your true purpose.

Your next step along the Yellow Brick Road is to love your friends. Remember, they are born in fire. They protect you so you don't feel so much pain. But as the fledgling must leave the nest, the Beautifully Bossy Leader must leave her friends behind, at least some of the time. Before you do that, it's important to connect to gratitude. This is how you integrate and celebrate these parts of yourself into an authentic whole.

Write the names of your four Bossy Friends. Next to each one, write down what they've done for you and why you're grateful to them.

Friend	Why I'm Grateful
_____	_____
_____	_____
_____	_____
_____	_____

Now that you've identified your friends and given them voices, who's left? Who is this person thanking them? Some who have gone through this process don't have an easy answer. Is that the case for you? If so, and if you were to choose a name for your authentic self, what would it be? You are the author of your Beautifully Bossy Leadership style. I encourage you to push limits and judgments to the side as you explore such questions. You can choose your own path down this Yellow Brick Road that we're following together.

As we saw in Chapter 15, a major guiding force in this process is purpose. I want you to write your purpose on this line as clearly and concisely as you can:

Integrating Your Authentic Self

_____
_____
_____

Did you struggle? Is your sense of purpose well-defined? If you could strengthen it, what changes would you make? The answers to these questions may come easily. They may not. Either way, it's okay. The inquiry itself is valuable. It places you on a journey of discovery. It fuels your curiosity. Being curious is an essential mindset for the Beautifully Bossy Leader. It will serve you as we move toward the final stretch of our journey and the important work that awaits us there.

If you can't come up with a clear answer, take a guess. Answer the question as though you were talking about someone else. If you had to guess what that person's purpose was, what would it be? Try that answer on for size. As you go forward, you are, of course, free to modify your response.

We are heading into the last phase of our work together. It will be the hardest. It will be worth it. It's time to put on our big-girl pant. We have some battling to do!

Part FOUR

— Seventeen —
Breaking the Grip of Fear

I was raised to be an independent woman, not the victim of anything.
Kamala Harris

We are now approaching that part of the **Yellow Brick Road** that's filled with wicked witches and flying monkeys. We will work together with our four friends to defeat forces that desperately keep you from being whole and claiming all of your personal power. You are stronger than the opposition. When you and your friends are aligned, you will achieve your purpose. Keep your resolve and nothing can stop you.

Take a long, revitalizing breath. There are four major forces (we will call them *bosses*) that impede our progress. We are going to break their hold, smash their power, and free your authentic self! We have talked at length about courage. What stands between you and full access to your Bossy Courage? Who is this culprit that holds us back in nearly everything?

Meet Boss Fear

When I picture Boss Fear, I think of him as big, strong, and imposing, like Bowser in the Mario games. He towers over you with menacing spikes, fiery breath, and a thunderous roar. What makes him particularly frightening is his relentless pursuit of you through every challenge of life, creating a tense and heart-pounding showdown. With each step closer to Bowser, the intensity builds, making your encounter with fear a nerve-wracking test of skill. Truth be told, though, his bark is always worse than his bite. At his core, he is a wimp. He can only hurt you if you let him.

Fear has an important biological function, of course, but in leadership, more often than not, it's worse than useless. It stops, distracts, inhibits, and restricts vision. It's the thing that keeps us from having important but difficult conversations. It's the factor that keeps us from taking chances, even when the reward far outweighs the risk. It's what keeps us from wholeness. Boss Fear must be put in his proper place. Here's the good news: There is a life hack that works every time you use it! Do you want to know what it is? GO. Literally, you must start.

Make a choice and then act on it. Use your power. When you do, Boss Fear shrinks.

The First Big Boss Battle: Boss Fear!

Step One: Write the name of the friend who teaches you Bossy Courage, the one analogous to my Wounded Weslyn: _____. This friend is crucial in this leg of your journey. Ask that friend a question: *What scares you the most and why?*

Write your friend's response:

_____
_____
_____
_____
_____

Step Two: Now go to a mirror and have an honest conversation with _____ (Write the name of the friend you identified above). Look in the mirror and talk directly to your friend. The first thing I want you to say is this: *Thank you. Thank you for protecting me from the dangers I have faced. Thank you for all of the pain you have endured on my behalf. I see you. I am grateful for you. I love you.* Enjoy this conversation, and let it flow. If tears come, let them fall. And if the experience isn't overly emotional, that's okay too. Practice the exercise anyway, and allow space for your friend to be seen. This friend has put everything into protecting you. Even if it feels like you have paid a price, maybe even a high one, your well-being and safety have always been this friend's number-one priority. Honest, heartfelt gratitude is appropriate and deserved. Go ahead, do it now.

Step Three: Think about the dangers that occupy your friend and how she consistently tries to keep you safe when you consider something difficult or risky. Ask yourself: could the action you're considering directly cause someone to die or suffer an injury? Are you really, really sure? Is this something you know, or do you just suspect it? If you have enough information to be sure that death or injury could happen, heed the warning. Do not act until circumstances change. If no one is going to die or be brutally harmed, go to the next step.

Step Four: The next thing to tell your friend is this: *While I understand that danger is real and important, it is NOT the most important thing. What's most important is my purpose and putting my gifts in the service of others.* Tell your friend about your purpose, mission, and the people involved. Tell _____ how much will be lost if those fears keep you from taking action. Tell your friend how much will be gained when you act despite those fears. Again, do it right now. You can say it in the mirror, or you can write it down. Nothing is more important at this moment.

Step Five: It's time to make a deal. Here are the terms: *You promise your friend that you will pay attention to the danger. In turn, your friend promises to stay out of the* *way*. When it's time to take an action that scares _____, she agrees she won't fight for the wheel. Your friend must allow you to drive in order to serve the greater purpose and the people you can positively impact.

What happened? Did your friend agree? If not, talk it through until you see eye-to-eye on this matter. It's not negotiable. Assure your friend that if the risks become real and tip the balance away from the gains, you will be glad for their help. Continue this conversation until you reach agreement.

Sometimes our friends surprise us with how they react. Respect their 'responses,' and give them real consideration. They may have valid points that should shape your actions. Just make sure you don't over-deliberate. Ultimately, the future is unknown. We must move forward with the faithful conviction that the best way we can positively affect outcomes is by placing our gifts at the service of others. As a Beautifully Bossy leader, your authentic self is best-equipped for this function. Keeping an open dialogue with your friends will help you overcome Boss Fear more consistently.

Early in my career, I worked in victim services. My responsibilities included being on call to respond to crime scenes, where I regularly witnessed the worst outcomes life has to offer. I wish I could say I was strong enough to maintain the perspective and professionalism to endure, but I wasn't. After a few years of being immersed in the grisly horror of murder and suffering, the job was killing my soul. While it was rewarding to function as a source of support for people in pain, I simply couldn't maintain my spirit and give the survivors all they deserved.

I needed to move away from the ugliness of violence for a new opportunity. Since the time I was four, my goal has been to be a motivational speaker. I found a high-profile training opportunity. I was the youngest and least experienced of thirty candidates, most of whom had advanced degrees in the field. I knew it was a long shot, but I had the confidence of knowing that I was born for the role.

The interview went as well as could be expected—until the end. I asked about their evaluation process and the remaining steps. The senior official replied, "Don't worry, sweetie. We'll get back to you when we're ready." While shaking hands, I responded, "I'm going to let you slide this time. But when you hire me because I'm the most qualified person for this job, I will never let you call me sweetie again." The man was shocked, and I was escorted out. What he didn't know was that I had already witnessed the bottom end of what life can offer, at my time in victim services. Not getting my dream job didn't compare to people dying. I had not realized until that moment that fear had very little grip on me unless life was on the line.

Breaking the Grip of Fear

Even still, I became nauseous. How could I have been so stupid? I cried in my car, certain that I had blown my opportunity.

What I didn't know was that the number-one quality the panel was searching for was professional courage. What I thought had been a fatal mistake was the very action that resulted in landing my dream job.

When you feel fear and take the right action anyway, you can rejoice! You may not always succeed, but when you are aligned with your purpose, honest and brave action most often wins the day. You have come a long way down the Yellow Brick Road. The ability to act irrespective of fear, granted through Bossy Courage, releases Boss Fear's debilitating grip and grants you access to your personal power. You will be qualified as a Beautifully Bossy Leader through your courageous willingness to take risks and put your people first. Congratulations! It is one of the greatest accomplishments available!

— Eighteen —
Dropping Our Masks

It's not about perfection.
It's about purpose.
Beyoncé

Defeating Boss Fear is a major milestone. If you haven't done it yet, have patience. Keep at it. You can do it! When you feel you have, celebrate by doing something nice for yourself. Maybe something Boss Fear has been keeping from you! You deserve it. You are well on your way to Beautiful Bossiness.

There is something else I want to tell you before we get on with our work. You defeated Boss Fear with Bossy Courage. You did it by taking action in spite of your fear. That doesn't mean Boss Fear is gone. He's just lost some of his power over you. You will face him again and again. The Beautifully Bossy Leadership Model is a cycle. You complete one level; you move up one, and the difficulty increases. With each encounter, you grow stronger and better able to meet the next challenge. You manifest more and more of your personal power.

Are you ready to take on the Level Two Boss? This one is a trickster. Of the four Bosses, this one can be the hardest to identify, pin down, and get past. Most of us have to do some intense work on ourselves to break this Boss's hold. He is clever, a master of deception. He convinces you that you are better off—safer—if you do as he says. What is this Boss's name?

Meet Boss Impostor

Boss Impostor reminds me of Jafar from *Aladdin*. He masquerades as a loyal advisor to the Sultan while secretly plotting his own ascent to power. With his sinister schemes and deceptive charm, he misleads those around him, cloaking his true intentions in a facade of loyalty and obedience. But behind his polished exterior lies the heart of a conniving imposter, ready to manipulate and betray for his own selfish ambitions.

Boss Impostor plays upon a deep-seated need to be seen, accepted, and valued by others. Human beings possess an inherent need for acceptance—longing to be recognized, valued, and embraced by others. This primal desire for approval and belonging drives social interactions, shapes relationships, and influences behavior. The need for acceptance is so deeply embedded, we

Dropping Our Masks

will devote nearly all of our energy to maintain it. Boss Impostor knows this and uses it against us.

He does this with sophisticated lies. He convinces us we will not achieve acceptance unless we heed him. In some cases, the promise of acceptance or approval may even tempt us to compromise our integrity or authenticity, leading to deceitful behavior to fit in. The ultimate price is the erosion of trust, strained relationships, and the loss of one's sense of self-worth. When we wear this mask that is deceitful at worst or disingenuous at best, we can experience immediate benefit. The problem is that over time, we forget we are wearing a mask. Even when the mask is no longer providing a benefit, we continue to wear it. That's because Boss Impostor convinces us that the masks we wear are not masks at all. He wants us to believe his mask has become our face.

That is exactly what he did to me. I thought I WAS Perfect Pearl, the good girl who was perfect and would never disappoint. But this notion of perfection can never truly be attained. I am flawed by nature, and our imperfections are an integral part of what makes us beautiful. Despite our best efforts, we will inevitably fall short of the unrealistic standards set by ourselves and others. My inability to see through the mask to the heart of me was an insurmountable barrier keeping me from genuine connection, forgiveness, and unconditional love. I never understood why I felt so alone. This lack of awareness kept me from breaking Boss Impostor's spell. For me, the only way through the barrier was a random auto accident and a physical blow to my brain. My injury stripped me of all of Pearl's pretense. I was no longer the perfect mother, the successful and independent businesswoman, or the pillar of granite against which all around me could lean. Those illusions were shattered. In their place was a vulnerable, dependent, broken, and about as far from perfect person as I could imagine.

And then, sitting in that dark room with nothing but silence to keep me company for months, I had a revelation.

Perfect Pearl's purpose and illusions had been forcibly stripped away. The mask was gone; I was incapable of perfection, but I **did not** experience the horrors Boss Impostor threatened. Instead of rejection, judgment, disappointment, and pain, I experienced more love, support, and acceptance than ever before. One of Boss Imposter's most powerful lies was exposed. He had convinced me it was *what I did and how I did it* that mattered to people. This is close to the truth, but not quite right. My worth was not only based upon my deeds— however clever, well-thought-out, or beyond expectation they might be. The people around me were better served when I could just BE. When I did that, and *only* that, I experienced overwhelming love and acceptance.

I had fancied myself an authentic person, but until Perfect Pearl lost sway, I had not fully found my authentic self. With authenticity within my grasp, I realized that without it I could not fully serve the needs of others. The mask had no value.

No matter how accomplished we become and no matter what impressive achievements we claim, Boss Impostor can still hold sway if we don't realize our purpose isn't only about us! Purpose comes from placing our natural gifts in the service of others.

There is even a common condition with this Boss's name: *Impostor Syndrome*. It's most often applied to high-performing women who—no matter how successful, competent, or brilliant—still feel inadequate. They feel like frauds who haven't earned their positions, and they fear being uncovered. We hold ourselves back when we persistently doubt our abilities, fear we don't deserve our achievements, or attribute our successes to luck rather than our own competence. Boss Imposter tells us we are unworthy of our position because there are others who could do it better. It's a crock! Of course, somebody COULD do it better. But they didn't. YOU did. The 'what if' game is a waste of energy, and Boss Impostor is the only one who wants us to play it.

There are ways to grow beyond the reach of Boss Impostor. We have already pointed to one powerful option—shifting from a self-focused mindset to one of servant leadership. It is a transformative journey of prioritizing the needs of others above one's own. It begins with a shift in perspective, moving away from a world of comparison toward a genuine desire to serve and support. Have you ever heard the saying, "Fake it 'till you make it?" This is exactly where we need to start sometimes. The mission, our loved ones, and our community need us to put one foot in front of the other, heal, and begin a different kind of introspection devoted to gratitude. When we embrace humility, empathy, and stewardship, servant leaders inspire trust and foster a sense of belonging. The leader's selfless dedication drives collective success. Moreso, this collective success and the process of serving provides leaders the self-worth we seek. When we internalize this, Boss Impostor loses his power.

The Second Big Boss Battle: Boss Imposter!

This exercise will be emotionally demanding, especially the first part, but it will smash Boss Impostor's hold by exposing his lies. First, we will see what his threats are really made of. Then, we will see how paper-thin and deceptive his threats truly are.

Step One: Self-Criticism Inventory. On the left side of the sheet, write down every self-criticism you can possibly think of. Be ruthless. Include past failures and ways people criticized you. Keep going until you can think of no more.

Step Two: The Whole-Hearted Truth. On the right side of the sheet, we're going to mount the argument for the defense. How would your best friend, your *true* best friend—the person, either real or imagined, who sees the real you—defend you from each of those criticisms? Write their counterarguments, and go into detail about why each criticism is, at best, only partially true.

Self-Criticism Inventory	The Whole-Hearted Truth

Are you okay? When I completed this exercise, I needed more than one piece of paper. I wrote things like *You're disgusting,* and *Your work will never mean anything to the world.* I'm guessing you've written similar doubt-based judgments. It's hard stuff. It's painful to recall. You are not alone, my sister. We have all lived with the lies listed in the left column.

Luckily, a rainbow hangs over these pages. When you wrote these words you released them from the prison within your heart and mind. Like many other things in life, the unknown and unspoken problems lurking in the darkness are the most difficult to face and fight. You just turned on the light with the truth—the whole-hearted truth—in the right column. That's the truth that comes from love and from the recognition that you are innately beautiful. You are valuable beyond any monetary measure.

A big part of becoming Bossy is shattering Boss Impostor's prison of shame, guilt, and blame, by embracing who we truly are. Like all of us—you have work to do to become the best version of yourself. But your beautiful gifts are meant to serve a purpose, to serve your neighbors, and to provide a path to wholehearted authenticity.

There is only one more thing to do to defeat Boss Impostor. Embrace purpose. When we live our purpose out loud, we show our authentic selves to the world. That is liberating, but it does not mean you go unopposed. It's not all rainbows and sunshine. Sometimes people will rain on our parades. That happens to me often because my purpose includes throwing challenges in front of people. And that's okay. Authenticity is about being vulnerable and opening ourselves to the judgment of others. It's about removing masks and letting ourselves be hurt to remain in line with what we value most. This is Beautifully Bossy.

— Nineteen —
Judgment Is for the Birds

One of life's greatest lessons is to stop judging and start having compassion for yourself and others.
Amanda Gore

This chapter was the most difficult to write because it's the part of this journey where I struggle the most. Writing about grace has changed my life forever. So many of you are already immeasurably graceful, and I have so much I can learn from you. But some of you are still barreling through life being bossy—with a lowercase b!

Our opponent as we walk in Bossy Grace is, for me, the most intimidating. Maybe it's because she isn't an obvious villain. There is no drool, no fangs. She moves elegantly through the world. As you watch her, you cannot help but wonder what it might be like to *be* her.

You may even want to be on her side to gain the benefits she flaunts. Who is this enigmatic antagonist?

Meet Boss Judgment

Boss Judgment reminds me of Meryl Streep's Miranda Priestly in *The Devil Wears Prada*. She is the Queen Bee. With her cutting remarks and exacting standards, she commands fear and respect in equal measure. Miranda's sharp tongue and critical eye spare no one, as she ruthlessly evaluates her employees and the fashion world at large. Her demeanor is icy and unapologetic, conveying an aura of superiority. Miranda's relentless pursuit of perfection and her willingness to sacrifice personal relationships for professional success paint her as a formidable antagonist, embodying the dark side of ambition and power. Everything is a show. It's all about appearance, but her beauty is shallow.

Boss Judgment issues swift, harsh sentences. Under her influence, we judge everybody and everything, including ourselves. Have you ever wondered why reality shows are popular? It can feel good to see others in 'train-wreck' situations and think, "I might have problems, but at least I'm not like that!"

The Third Big Boss Battle: Boss Judgment!

How do you defeat Boss Judgment? My answer comes from my leadership development practice and from successfully helping leaders over the last two decades. We must consider how Boss Judgment uses her measuring stick. Lording over your shoulder, her clever critiques are based on your propensity to see yourself in one of two ways. Defeating her; therefore, requires two very different strategies. For that reason, we need to divide this chapter into two tracks. You will choose the one that is right for you.

Do you find that you are typically better than most people you know, or do you tend to see others as better than you? I want you to answer honestly because you need to choose the right approach as we take on Boss Judgment together. If you don't, the work ahead may hurt more than it helps.

This is not a comfortable question to consider. I get that. We must learn to accept things as they are without judgment. One path is neither better or worse than the other. Each has its advantages and disadvantages.

There are various models to describe this aspect of human behavior. One of the most powerful I've encountered is David McClelland's Human Motivation Theory. In his research, David McClelland found that people are motivated in three primary ways:

1. **Power (Personalized or Socialized):** Enjoys status and influencing others for either personal gain or the greater good. Tends to be found in

high-level positions and can be highly revered or deeply despised, depending on which type of power is sought.

2. **Achievement:** Enjoys personal accomplishment and promotion potential. Tends to be found in positions where success is solely dependent on personal effort.
3. **Affiliation:** Enjoys belonging to a group and harmonious social interactions. Tends to be found in positions where collaboration and safety are the norm.

Our motivations profoundly influence our decision-making and leadership styles. Understanding this is essential as we face Boss Judgment head-on. Why? Because Boss Judgment speaks to us through what we value most. If power moves you more than affiliation, Boss Judgment will tell you that you can always have *more* power. If you are more prone to seeking affiliation, Boss Judgment will tell you how you can better 'fit in.' Please refer to the next graph:

Measuring Stick

Power - Risk   Affiliation - Safety
Confidence   **Humility**
Leadership style uses accountability   Leadership style uses appreciation

Beautifully Bossy Leadership is the mature balance between:
Confidence and Humility
Accountability and Appreciation
Risk and Safety

To the right, we have increasing humility. To the left, increasing confidence. Of course, humility and confidence are both good things. Beautifully Bossy Leaders need both. But we also have the inverse—decreasing confidence to the right, decreasing humility to the left. This is where blind spots in our approach to leadership come into play. It's the way Boss Judgment can keep us from achieving Bossy Grace.

Let's divide into our two tracks: Eagles and Geese. Regardless of the track for you, the goal for the Beautifully Bossy Leader is always to find a balance between confidence and humility. This is crucially important in the art of leadership. When you find and maintain this balance you can effectively lead others. If you don't, inefficient chaos and/or paralyzing fear will infect your organization. Have you ever wondered why no one willingly approaches you when they've made a mistake? Or have you realized that no matter what you do, people go in many directions and don't accomplish anything? You're not alone. You're tipped too far on one side of the measuring stick! In balance, you know when and how to use the carrot of appreciation and the stick of accountability.

As I write these words, I realize more than ever how I must grow in Bossy Grace. We cannot just snap our fingers and—*poof!*—we're graceful. No, we are given opportunities to build where we must. My friend, Marvelous Mommy, is the one who provided the opportunity for Bossy Grace and humility to grow in my heart.

During my first eleven years of motherhood, I was certain I was the most incredible mother ever. I looked down on parents with out-of-control children. I gagged with disgust as I watched friends helplessly remind their children that drinking out of the toilet-brush holder wasn't safe. I judged . . . *hard.*

God decided it was my turn to learn humility when sweet, independent, headstrong, beautiful, 'persuasive' Korinna blew up my world and my illusion of superiority. My confidence was a casualty. This process didn't feel like a gift, nor did it seem like an opportunity for growth, but the journey toward becoming Korinna's mom has been one of the greatest gifts I have ever received. My mask of perfection was left smoldering on the ground as my love for her was so fierce it was impossible to give up and walk away. I had no choice but to continue as a perfectly imperfect mommy to the beautiful baby who is the only person in my life more independent than I am!

Which brings us to the meat of this chapter. What was your answer to my question? If you feel like you are better in general than others, then you are probably like me. You need to work on building humility in the Eagles track. **Go to Chapter Nineteen (A).** If you feel like others are better than you in general, you will benefit by building confidence and skipping ahead to the Geese track. **Go to Chapter Nineteen (B).**

— Nineteen (A) —
Eagle Track

Eagles fly high and solo. They are dangerous with sharp talons. The way of the Eagle involves risk, especially during opportunities to increase power. They are disruptive. Disruption is the catalyst for innovation, challenging the status quo, and driving progress, but it does not promote peace and harmony. Our friends, the geese, want nothing to do with the chaos that we bring to the table. Often a lonely path detached from other people, effective Eagles know; however, that they are not powerful enough to accomplish big missions on their own. Therefore, to be successful, they must learn balance.

Eagle-style leaders lead with power that can translate into fear-based threats. Followers do not thrive under those conditions. When there is no trust, deep loyalty, or commitment, the shared mission and feeling of purpose become out of reach.

Eagle Exercise

To grow as a Beautifully Bossy leader, the way of the Eagle means growth in humility. This exercise could be harmful or dangerous for you or others if used improperly. It's important to rein in our confidence but not destroy it. A word of **warning:** If you fall on the Geese side of the scale, please skip this exercise and accept the biggest hug from me instead!

Step One: People Watching. I want you to purposefully awaken Boss Judgment by going to a public place where there is a wide mix of people and write down all the judgments you can about them. Describe in detail what you notice and how that makes you feel. Make at least a dozen entries.

	Boss Judgment says?	Unprejudiced Description of What You See
1		
2		
3		
4		
5		
6		
7		
8		
9		
10		
11		
12		

Step Two: Analysis. At home, look over your list. Look for patterns. Are there any commonalities? Write them down.

_____

_____

Do you feel some judgments more intensely than others?

_____

_____

Do you feel somehow superior to those people? Why? Write down those too.

_____

_____

Have you noticed themes? What are they? Are any of them relevant to things you may have thought about yourself in the past?

_____

_____

Let's go one step further. Try to answer each question.

What makes you better than them?

_____

_____

Why do you think that?

_____

_____

Are you sure? Why do you care?

_____

_____

Finish this exercise before reading further.

Done? Okay. Now I am going to tell you the actual answers to the last three questions. What makes you better than them? **You are not.** How do you know that? **You do not.** Why do you care? **You should not.**

Hey there. Are you okay? Mad at me? A little irritated with these stupid exercises? I get it. I'm right there with you. It took me many years and one of the best servant leaders in the world by my side to get through answering these kinds of questions. Sometimes our wounding encourages us to fly higher and alone (act overly confident and arrogant) so that no one notices our determined yet joyless faces. We appear confident but are concealing soft underbellies and vulnerabilities. Our survival instincts kick in, and we draw upon our resilience to demonstrate a sense of poise and assurance. OR . . . maybe it's just me, and you are just so damn good that no one else has ever been able to keep up!?! ☺

Either way, I love you, and I believe in you. The connection and whole-heartedness you desire is worth the mud and muck you'll wade through to get there. You are not alone. Not anymore.

Go to Chapter Nineteen (C).

— Nineteen (B) —
Geese Track

I always wanted to join the Geese side, or at least be able to walk undetected amongst the geese. I never seem to fit in with large groups of friends. Such groups perceive me as threatening, even when I wholeheartedly seek love and belonging. It makes me sad.

Abraham Maslow's Hierarchy of Needs tells us we all require love and belonging to ascend to our greatest self. Geese are naturals at that. Have you ever watched actual geese? They have perfected the utility of community. They migrate in V formations, taking turns leading from the front. Why? The aerodynamics of the V formation make the arduous task of flying thousands of miles easier for the entire group. If one goose falls out of formation, for any reason, another goose will stay to make sure they have the best possible chance to catch up. The currency for Geese is affiliation, and it pays the dividends of safety and a sense of belonging. The way of the Geese represents a stabilizing force, one that strives to maintain harmony and connection within organizations.

Geese-style leaders tend to employ a democratic, inclusive approach. They use appreciation as their emotional currency. This might feel good in the short term, but it leads to organizational chaos in the long term. Without accountability, mediocrity becomes the norm. People feel like there's no real direction and resent others who do not pull their weight. Confusion about the mission and an ill-defined sense of purpose will reduce the group's energetic contributions, which is the lifeblood of any organization.

No matter how strong your humility or how low your confidence, I know you sometimes want to be seen. Sometimes, you need power and influence, especially if you're going to be the best Beautifully Bossy Leader you can be! Here's how I encourage you to proceed:

Geese Exercise

Step One: Brainstorm. On the left side of the chart below, capture as many ideas as you can for Strengths and Opportunities. Really think this through. If you struggle, think about what the people who love you might say.

Strengths are positive internal factors. To make your list, answer: What are your greatest assets? What do people love about you? What do you love about yourself? Make as many entries as you can.

Opportunities are positive external factors. To make your list, consider this: How can you use your strengths to make a difference in the world, for others, or to accomplish a mission? Who do you know who would like to see you succeed? Make as many entries as you can.

Now, move to the right side. You may only list three weaknesses and three threats.

Weaknesses are negative internal factors. To identify your list of three, answer this: What prevents you from being the best version of yourself?

Threats are negative external factors. To identify your list of three, answer this: Who or what stands in the way of your purpose?

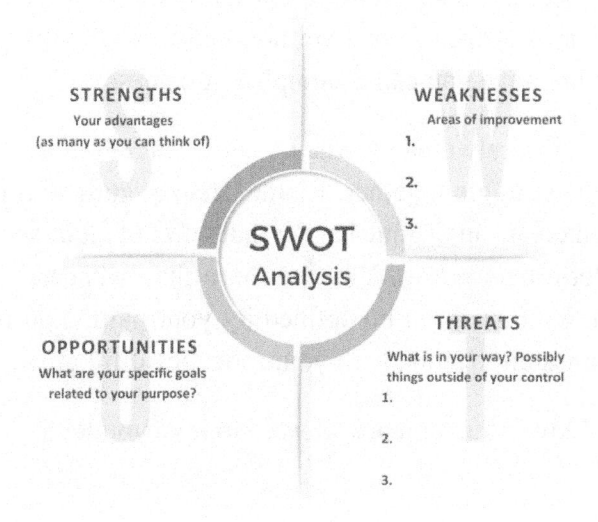

STRENGTHS
Your advantages
(as many as you can think of)

WEAKNESSES
Areas of improvement
1.
2.
3.

SWOT Analysis

OPPORTUNITIES
What are your specific goals related to your purpose?

THREATS
What is in your way? Possibly things outside of your control
1.
2.
3.

After you have completed the chart, review it with a trusted partner. Challenge them to add at least three more items to the categories on the left side and cross off one from the right side. Ask them to explain why. (You can blame me and tell them I am making you do it!)

Step Two: Analysis. Look at the completed chart. Are you surprised by any of it? Were you at all shocked to see how much you truly bring to the table? Girl, this is what is true—you were made to be beautiful. You were made to be purposeful. And you were made to make a difference with your love and leadership.

My guess is you breathe life into everyone around you. People feel your love and are drawn by the peace they feel from you. You might not believe me yet, but you are a work of art. I am honored to walk with you, and I believe you can accomplish greatness.

I sincerely mean it when I say we are all in the self-image struggle together. Blame, shame, guilt, and pain often create an opaque barrier that will not let us see out or let others see in. You are more than what has hurt you. You need not be defined by your pain. You have permission to shine with your most beautiful glow.

I love you. You are allowed to love you too.

— Nineteen (C) —
Leaders of All Styles

Whether you identify as an Eagle or a Goose, Boss Judgment always looking over your shoulder. She applies her measuring stick between you and others and between you and your best version of yourself. Boss Judgment creates loneliness, heartache, paralysis, and doubt. But she has one fatal weakness. She can never act alone. She can only impede your purpose and your mission with your permission. She only has power if you give it to her. Her existence depends upon on ability to convince you she IS you. If she cannot, she is nothing more than a shadow.

How do you keep yourself from fueling her, giving her power, and disrupting the balance that gives you your personal power?

We dismiss judgment by curing ignorance and building maturity. We build space for thinking, space for difference, space for curiosity. This is where the skills of emotional intelligence come into play. When you notice Boss Judgment's presence, take some time and use some space to respond rather than merely reacting in a kneejerk way. Flying off the handle is not a balanced behavior. When you feel an emotional charge, a useful habit is to inquire first and comment later. For instance, instead of judging, say, "I really want to understand what you're saying. Can you tell me more?"

During confrontations, think about what you really want or need, *as it relates to your purpose and the shared mission*. Is any given situation worth losing a friend or a direct report or a job? What is the ideal solution? What will move you in that direction? This is the sort of discipline that defines high emotional intelligence, and it's been positively correlated to high-performing executives. This is no accident. Bossy Grace grows in the absence of Boss Judgment, and it makes fertile ground for healthy development in all of life's relationships.

— Twenty —
It's Not About You!

At the end of the day, it's not about what you have or even what you've accomplished... It's about who you've lifted up, who you've made better. It's about what you've given back.
Denzel Washington

How are you feeling, my friend? I know this journey has been emotionally challenging. Are you feeling free from the steely grips of Boss Fear, Boss Impostor, and Boss Judgment? At least a little? If so, that's wonderful! If that is not yet your experience, please don't be discouraged. These Bosses are strong. They didn't take control overnight, and it takes time and a concerted effort to loosen their grip.

When you feel ready, I encourage you to soldier on through one last battle. You have proven you can do this work. You are up to the challenge. And you're not alone. Together, we've got this. I also want to make sure you know what you're in for. This last Boss, for most of us, is the most formidable. She is ruthless. She doesn't want a little from you. She wants *everything*. And everything isn't enough. She is the one who keeps us from manifesting Bossy Love.

Meet Boss Ego

I picture Boss Ego as Ursula from *The Little Mermaid*. Ursula opposes Ariel, so maybe that's no accident. Exploiting others' desires for her own gain, she preys upon their weaknesses, offering false promises in exchange for their souls. With her grandiose ego and relentless pursuit of domination, Ursula stops at nothing to satisfy her own ambitions, casting aside empathy and compassion in favor of her twisted desires for control and supremacy.

Throughout these pages, we have talked about power. We need to be clear about power, because it comes in different forms. We referred to McClelland's identification of power as a motivating factor. He spoke of personalized power, the desire for influence over others. This is not the kind of power we're building. When *we* talk about personal power, we mean the power within ourselves. It's the ability to look inside ourselves with courage and clarity. It's the ability to choose what we know is right. Personal power gives us access to our

It's Not About You!

potential because it is through resolve and discipline that we develop our natural gifts.

This is not the power Boss Ego craves. She wants power over others—to harm them. Power over ourselves helps us and allows us to serve others. This is why my mentors relentlessly beat the *It's not about you!* drum. They were trying to help me beat Boss Ego. *That* is Bossy Love.

The Fourth Big Boss Battle: Boss Ego!

You know how to manifest your personal power by developing the four Bossy Values. Your friends help you, primarily by showing you what those values are not. As you gain personal power, Boss Ego's influence diminishes—Bossy Love is the reward.

Bossy Love is distinct from the other Bossy Values. It's really all about action and sacrifice. It has nothing to do with emotion. Remember how we defined it—prioritizing others' needs above our own desires. This is good news because we can defeat Boss Ego by taking action—repeated, valuable action. We can DECIDE to embody Bossy Love.

Bossy Love is sacrifice. Always. Here's an example: My company worked with an executive team. Tammi, one of the senior executives, was given a directive from her boss to conduct a negative performance review on Angie, one of her direct reports. In Tammi's view, this was undeserved. Angie had been her mentor in the past. Tammi considered Angie one of the most valuable people in the organization, but Angie had fallen out of favor with those above Tammi. Someone was going to fall on the sword, either Tammi or Angie, and it was Tammi's call. Tammi felt she simply could not risk losing her job. She did as she was told.

Angie reacted as you might expect. After a tearful confrontation, Tammi apologized deeply and swore she would make it right. At the next staff meeting, Tammi stood in front of the entire management team, Angie included, and she praised Angie and apologized for signing and delivering an undeserved assessment. In that moment, Tammi became my hero. She lived Bossy Love out loud and did the right thing despite the consequences. Tammi did pay a price. She lost her job, but she did not lose her integrity. She mustered the personal power to do what was right. Her team would have followed her anywhere, and they did. She just completed the dissertation for her doctorate and she's having an even greater impact on the world in her new position.

Bossy Love often sucks! I mean it when I tell you Bossy Love puts others' needs first and our own wishes last. Being a real leader means going first even when you know you could take enemy fire. When you choose Bossy Love, your life is no longer about you. It's about the mission. It's about your people.

It's Not About You!

Bossy Love is not soft. Sometimes the right thing is the hard thing. Sometimes, as leaders, we must serve the organization's health. Because without that, the shared mission is doomed. Decisions made in your own best interest are from a place of personalized power and flow from the influence of that evil octopus, Boss Ego. Bossy Love makes the choice of the mission first, my people second, me last. When you make this choice, all of your relationships (family, team, organization) will thrive. I promise.

Let's see how you may have already experienced Bossy Love and true leadership.

Bossy Love and Leadership Exercise #1

Step One: Identify the two most influential people in your life. One of them can be a parent or primary caretaker, but if so, the other must not be. Write their names below and list as many of their characteristics and attributes as you can. Use as many adjectives as you need to describe their impact on you.

Influencer #1:	Influencer #2:

Step Two: Analysis. Look over your list.

What overall description would you give to each of these people?

Influencer #1:
_____

Influencer #2:
_____

How are they set apart from others in your life?

Influencer #1:
_____

Influencer #2:
_____

Did they put your needs ahead of their own desires? How? What did they give up?

Influencer #1:
_____

Influencer #2:
_____

How do you feel now? Do you have a better picture of what Bossy Love in action looks like? Good, because the next step is for you to make a specific action plan to better embody Bossy Love and leadership.

Bossy Love and Leadership Exercise #2

Identify three people to whom you will provide true leadership. They can be a part of any area of your life but choose at least one person in your personal life and one in your professional life.

Person #1: _____

Person #2: _____

Person #3: _____

Identify goals to help them fulfill their most pressing needs. Remember, goals are most powerful when they are clear, so make them SMART: Specific, Measurable, Achievable, Relevant, and Time-bound. As you complete the following chart, remember that Bossy Love involves sacrifice. Doing so, you are saying goodbye to Boss Ego and hello to your Beautifully Bossy Leadership style.

I Will be a Beautifully Bossy Leader for:

	Person 1	Person 2	Person 3
Specific What need will I help them meet? Why is this important? What is my goal?			
Measurable How will I know I have succeeded?			
Achievable What's in the way? Can I reasonably get past it?			
Relevant Will this serve a greater good? What could that mean?			
Time-bound When will this need be met?			
Bossy Love sacrifice What must I give up to help the person achieve their needs?			

It's Not About You!

We women have tendencies that help and hurt us as we grow in Bossy Love. What helps us is our compassion. Maybe it's the motherly instinct to provide for the needs of those we care about. Some of us also want to 'fix' other people. I'm guilty of this. We see their immense potential and want greatness for them more than they want it for themselves. We invest our time and energy in changing someone who doesn't want to change—an impossible goal. We can only control the actions of one person, ourselves. But through the power of Bossy Love, we create an environment that inspires people to change themselves. That is real leadership.

People who are free from Boss Ego are not in servitude, even though they serve. It seems counterintuitive. But if you live for yourself, when you die, you're just dead. If you lived Bossy Love, free from Boss Ego's grip, you lived for others, and you will live on in them after you pass away. Your real power is never gone. The ripple effects of what you caused will grow and multiply. You are a light in the world. Darkness cannot erase the light, but light always erases darkness. Tears come to my eyes as I remember Mikey, one of the most influential people in my life. Mikey's desire was the opposite of Ursula's. He

> "Love is Leadership and Leadership is Love."
>
> Bossy Bit #22

wanted to fill souls, not drain them. He has been gone for years now, but his power lives on. It lives through me. Now it lives through you.

— Epilogue —

My Love Letter to You

*And even I can't teach you how to fly,
but I can show you how to live
like your life is on the line.*
P!nk, "All I Know So Far"

Dearest Friend,

How are you? If you have made it this far, you have walked through some darkness and muck. As we conclude our time together, I want to take this opportunity to love you. This is a little note from my heart to yours. I hope you are willing to feel my words and let them fill your cup just a bit because now it's your turn. It's your turn to move into the world—bloodied, but not beaten; weary, but so very worthy; powerful, but not prideful—to fill the cups of the thousands of women whose lives you touch and who need your love.

Throughout history, women have been encouraged and even required to remain silent. The b-words are just one way to lower our voice, lessen our power, and impede our leadership. Our movement will ensure that never happens again.

You may wonder why I was willing to put all of my pain and shame on these pages for the world to see. Believe me, I've asked myself the same thing. I did it because someone must go first. Societal norms dictate that, professionally and personally, we are to be caregivers, nurturers, and supporters. We are taught to bury our pain and run from our shame so that we can be "lady-like." Our needs and desires are supposed to come after those of the people around us. Here we are, already silently screaming inside a prison of expectations, and this chick who calls herself the Bossy Girl is ALSO telling us to put ourselves last!?! Yeah right!!!

Here's the thing; servant leadership transcends the boundaries of gender and allows us an equal playing field previously not accessible to us. We now have a tool (a way of being) at our fingertips. In this way of being, we are naturally inclined to excel. It is a leadership style that will build trust and loyalty, stronger relationships, and higher levels of engagement. We can encourage open communication, collaboration, and innovation. And we have the edge! Servant leadership is the secret to increasing not only your effectiveness, but also your reputation. There will be no more balancing between nice enough and too pushy. It's no longer personal. It's not about you or about them. It's about the mission.

My mission was to love you and allow you the same opportunity I had to heal and love others. Like you, I have had my trials. It has been messy. It sometimes remains so. But we need to start somewhere.

I shared my story so you would know you are not alone. I want you to know that you are no less of a lady for being radically honest and courageous about who you are and who you are meant to be. Female leaders have spent far too long making themselves smaller to fit into boxes the world has created for us. At the tender age of six, girls begin to accept the belief that boys are stronger and smarter. To this day, when I facilitate training and divide the class into groups, it is the men who are selected to speak. If you don't know what I am talking about, be on the lookout. The next time you see a workgroup tasked with selecting a spokesperson, notice who is selected.

We must change this. When an opportunity is presented, raise your hand! We need to be proud to live and lead as women in our own right. Vote for your sister. Pull her chair right up to the boardroom table. That's Bossy!

It's a plain fact that if we want to lead others well and fulfill the purpose we were made for, we must walk through our own darkness first. We must face and defeat fear, masks, judgment, and ego. On the other side of that battle is your full power. It comes from an overflowing self-love that serves others and creates relationships that last lifetimes.

When I completed my thesis for my master's degree, I interviewed twenty incredibly influential female leaders: college presidents, doctors, attorneys, executives, business owners. One question I never asked in my interviews was about the relationship women have with one another. However, every single one of my interviewees talked about how women are each other's worst enemies.

Isn't that sad? We should be building each other up, not reinforcing tropes that have long outlived their relevance. Why would women not want to work for or hire another woman? The reason is that we haven't all done the work in this book? We all have shadows within ourselves that we have denied or suppressed. We struggle to love others and be vulnerable with our hearts and feelings. We need our full strength. When we can courageously investigate the darker parts and feel boldly grateful for every trauma that forged us into the women we are meant to be, everything changes. The sun comes out. We become prepared to achieve the purpose for which we were created. And when we become whole together, we create a wave.

With all of that said, there is one more thing. Growing in your mindset and your ability to lead and connect with others is NOT an academic exercise. You must DO something! Like Dorothy in Oz, you must take action. You need to do it now before you are immersed in the next big thing

Epilogue: My Love Letter to You

pulling you in a thousand directions. And there is more bad news. Change is not an event; it is a process and a cycle. You will have to choose action, choose love, choose courage, and choose leadership repeatedly. Like Dorothy, you will fall, and it will hurt. You will want to quit, but please don't quit.

Everyone knows that Dorothy returned to Kansas at the end of *The Wizard of Oz,* but if you read the books, you will discover that Dorothy gathered her family in Kansas and took them all to the colorful, marvelous Land of Oz. This is a movement, and the movement is bigger than me or you or any of us individually. Now that you have taken your journey and are becoming the Beautifully Bossy woman you were meant to be, it is time to help others do the same. This is the work that will fill that empty spot inside of you that says you are meant for more. This is your voice. This is your power. Keep choosing Bossy. For you. *Because you deserve this.*

Love Relentlessly,

BG

Meet Kristal, The Bossy Girl, author and leadership development consultant who penned her book while battling the very demons she courageously addresses within these pages. In 2021, amidst her struggles, she embarked on a journey of healing that she wrote about as it unfolded.

This photo captures Kristal in the heat of her battle, hands on her hips, ready for whatever challenge may come her way. Yet, when she shared this image on social media, it was met with apprehension and unease, echoing the societal discomfort often felt toward assertive (Bossy) women—a stereotype Kristal challenges head-on.

Just days before publication, the cover photo was taken. It's a reflection of Kristal today: poised, content, connected, and deeply loved. This image resonates differently, inviting you into Kristal's world of love in service—empowered, embodying the essence of her message.

Kristal's journey of transformation is not just her own; it's an invitation to you to embrace your power, lead with heart, and embark on your own path to healing. Through her words, she extends a hand of love and has faith that you will share that love with those around you. After all, as the Bossy Girl reminds us, your vulnerability is your strength, and your love is your legacy.

Made in the USA
Middletown, DE
12 May 2024